FAMOUS MINNESOTANS

Past and Present

Dan Flynn

NODIN PRESS

To my parents
Terry and Kathy Flynn

John Toren, Editor

Julie Tilka, Designer

Tom Van Asch, Photo Retouch

ISBN - 1-932472-29-0

Nodin Press is a division of Micawbers, Inc.
530 N. Third Street, Suite 120
Minneapolis, Minnesota 55401

Louie Anderson

THE APPLAUSE WAS SO GREAT after Louie Anderson's first appearance on *The Tonight Show* in 1984 that Johnny Carson called him back out. It must have been a dream come true.

Born in St. Paul in 1953, Anderson comes from a family of eleven kids. His family life gave him material for his life's work, which began as a stand-up comedian performing at colleges and clubs in the late 1970s and early 1980s. In fact, his career began almost spontaneously. He was visiting a comedy club with friends, and he declared that he was as funny as anyone who had appeared that evening on stage. His friends dared him to prove it—and he's been proving it ever since.

Anderson's career was given a big boost in 1981, when he won the first annual Midwest Comedy Competition. More important than winning the competition, Anderson impressed the emcee, legendary comic Henny Youngman. Youngman not only hired him as a joke writer, but also personally recommended him to Las Vegas clubs, where Anderson was soon working regularly.

Anderson's book, *Dear Dad: Letters from an Adult Child*, a bittersweet rendering of his experiences growing up with an alcoholic father, became a national best seller in 1991. He also appeared in *Coming to America*, *Ferris Bueller's Day Off*, and other films; but Anderson's biggest success was the cartoon series he cocreated with Matt O'Callaghan, *Life with Louie*. The popular Fox network series became the number-one Saturday morning cartoon in 1997, and Anderson won consecutive Emmys for Outstanding Performance in an Animated Series in 1996 and 1997.

A regular performer in Las Vegas clubs, and well known for his comedy specials on HBO and Showtime, Anderson began hosting the game show *Family Feud* in 1999. He appears regularly on late night TV to chat with Jay Leno and David Letterman, and in 2002 he published *The F Word: How to Survive Your Family*. In addition to his television and night club appearances Anderson performs every New Year's Eve at the University of Minnesota.

Follow Your Heart!

Jessica Lange

IN 1983 JESSICA LANGE became the first actress in more than forty years to receive two Oscar nominations in the same year. She was nominated for Best Actress for the movie *Frances* and for Best Supporting Actress for *Tootsie*.

Lange was born on April 20, 1949, in Cloquet, Minnesota. Her father was a traveling salesman and her family was constantly on the move. After graduating from Cloquet High School, Lange accepted an art scholarship to the University of Minnesota, but while still a freshman she fell in love with a visiting photography professor named Paco Grande, and left with him to "see the world." The couple eventually settled in New York City, where Grande worked on independent film projects. Inspired by a screening of the French film *Children of Paradise*, Lange moved to Paris to study mime and dance. By the time she returned to New York City two years later, the marriage had deteriorated, and when Grande left for Jamaica, Lange stayed behind and began to take acting classes. She supported herself by waiting tables in Greenwich Village and modeling for the Wilhelmina Agency. By a fluke of fortune, producer Dino DeLaurentiis contacted the agency looking for a fresh face for his remake of *King Kong* (1976)—and that's how Lange got her start in films.

Her performance in *King Kong* was not well received, however, and Lange returned to New York. Not long afterward she kindled a seven-year relationship with ballet star Mikhail Baryshnikov. Eventually, as a result of name exposure and screen tests, Lange began receiving film roles again. She appeared in Bob Fosse's *All That Jazz* (1979) and was cast alongside Jack Nicholson in *The Postman Always Rings Twice* (1981), where she astonished critics by a new-found depth and range of expression.

From that time on Lange has starred in many celebrated films, including *Frances, Tootsie, Sweet Dreams, Country, Crimes of the Heart, Blue Sky,* (for which she won an Academy Award for Best Actress), *Rob Roy,* and *Big Fish*. While continuing to make films and act in playhouses, Lange and actor-playwright Sam Shepard (with whom she became romantically involved in 1982) maintain a home in Stillwater, Minnesota, where they raise their children Hannah and Samuel.

In 1983 Jessica Lange became the first actress in more than forty years to receive two Oscar nominations in the same year. She was nominated for Best Actress for the movie *Frances* and for Best Supporting Actress for *Tootsie*.

JESSICA LANGE

THE POSTMAN ALWAYS RINGS TWICE

(1981) Jessica Lange stars opposite Jack Nicholson in this chilling film about adultery and murder.

FRANCES

(1982) Lange is nominated for a Best Actress Oscar for her stunning portrayal of actress Francis Farmer, whose career was derailed by personal problems.

TOOTSIE

(1982) In this romantic comedy Lange seems very Minnesotan as a shy, laid-back actress in New York. She received an Oscar for Best Supporting Actress. Costar Dustin Hoffman received a Best Actor nomination.

BLUE SKY

(1994) Lange wins her first Best Actress Oscar. In the film she plays a philandering yet earnest wife and mother.

LOSING ISAIAH

(1995) Lange plays a social worker who, along with her husband (David Strathairn), takes in an abandoned child, mistakenly left for dead by his crack addict mother (Halle Berry). Lange puts in a gritty performance during the long courtroom custody battle.

Ann Sothern

ANN SOTHERN WAS BORN as Harriet Lake in Valley City, North Dakota, on January 22, 1909. Her father left the family when she was six years old, and her mother moved to Minneapolis. Harriet learned to play the piano and attended Minneapolis Central High School. A talented singer, Lake had dreams of becoming a big star.

She began her film career in Hollywood as an extra in 1927 for MGM, appeared in a few prominent roles on Broadway, and was eventually signed by Columbia Picture to star in *Let's Fall in Love*. That same year, 1934, she appeared alongside Eddie Cantor in *Kid Millions*. For the next two years she starred in a string of B movies, and when Columbia dropped her she went on to a series of similarly modest films for RKO.

During the 1940s Sothern's career improved. She played the brassy Maisie in a series of films centered on that character (a part originally conceived for Jean Harlow) and she also starred in several features such as: *Cry Havoc*, *Letter to Three Wives*, *April Showers*, and *Words and Music*. With the arrival of television, Sothern starred for three years in the sitcom *Private Secretary* (1953–1957), and was later given her own *The Ann Sothern Show* (1958–1961), in which she played an office secretary.

In later life Sothern continued to appear sporadically in movies and television, including a role as the car's voice in *My Mother the Car*, and received an Oscar nomination for *The Whales of August* (1987) for her role as Trish Doughty.

Sothern died in 2002.

Peter Graves

PETER GRAVES PLAYED the role of Mr. Jim Phelps on the popular 1960s television show *Mission: Impossible*. He is the younger brother of actor James Arness. Arness is the family name.

Graves is from Minneapolis and attended the University of Minnesota. He has appeared in numerous film and television productions, the most notable of which are the movies *Stalag 17* and *Airplane*. He also appeared in the television show *Fury* and has hosted the *A & E Biography* series.

Since 1950 he has been married to Joan Endress. The couple has three daughters. As of 2002 Graves could be seen on television promoting Beltone hearing aids.

JAMES ARNESS

HIGH SCOOL

(1938–1941) Arness attends Minneapolis West and Washburn High Schools.

RADIO ANNOUNCER

(1945) After serving with the U.S. Army in Italy during World War II, Arness returns to Minneapolis and works as a radio announcer.

THE FARMER'S DAUGHTER

(1947) Arness plays Peter Holstrom, the brother of a Minnesota farm girl who moves to Washington, D.C. Loretta Young won a Best Actress Oscar for the role of Katie Holstrom.

GUNSMOKE

(1955–1975) John Wayne recommends James Arness for the role of Marshal Matt Dillon. The television series, which depicts life in Dodge City, Kansas, is a huge success, and becomes the longest-running television show of all time.

James Arness

JAMES ARNESS PLAYED the role of Marshal Matt Dillon on the popular television show *Gunsmoke* for twenty-one years.

Arness was born in Minneapolis in 1923. He is the older brother of actor Peter Graves. The future gunslinger attended Minneapolis Washburn and West high schools.

After serving in World War II, he worked in radio before moving to California, where he became a television star. The legendary actor John Wayne recommended Arness for the part of Marshal Matt Dillon.

Arness was nominated for an Emmy Award in 1956, but lost to Robert Young of *Father Knows Best*. Arness lost to Robert Young the following season as well. In 1959, the Emmy went to Raymond Burr of *Perry Mason*. *Gunsmoke* went off the air in 1975.

Tippi
Hedren

NATHALIE KAY HEDREN WAS born on January 19, 1931, in Lafayette, Minnesota. She worked as a model in Minneapolis before moving to New York City. Alfred Hitchcock caught sight of her in a commercial while watching *The Today Show*, and the next year he cast her in his thriller, *The Birds*. Hedren won the Best Newcomer Golden Globe Award for her portrayal of an innocent young woman in a tranquil town that is slowly being overrun by a flock of ravens. A year later she starred alongside Sean Connery in Hitchcock's *Marnie*. Hedren also appeared on television in the Kraft Suspense Theater.

Though she continued to make films, Hedren's acting career in time took a back seat to her other interests. She began to travel widely as a relief coordinator for Food for the Hungry, setting up programs for victims of famine, earthquakes, hurricanes, and war. She lobbied Congress on behalf of Asian refugees, which earned her a Humanitarian Award presented to her by the B'hai Faith. She entertained troops in Vietnam, and became very active in African wildlife preservation. In 1981 her lengthy film project on that theme, *The Roar*, was released. She later co-authored a book, *Shambala*, recounting the project, and founded the Shambala wildlife preserve outside of Los Angeles, California, to care for animals and provide an environment where visitors could appreciate the wild beasts, many of which were castoffs from circuses and zoos.

Hedren currently lives at Shambala in a cottage surrounded by pens containing cats of all sizes and descriptions. "I awaken to their roars," she says.

Tippi continues to work occasionally in films, television, and theater. She was honored in 1995 with a Life Achievement award from Spain's Fundacion Municipal De Cine, and in 1999 she was chosen as a "Woman of Vision" by Women of Film and Video in Washington, D.C.

Though she continued to make films, Hedren's acting career in time took a back seat to her other interests.

Cheryl Tiegs

CHERYL TIEGS WAS THE first supermodel.

Born in Breckenridge, Minnesota, on September 25, 1947, Tiegs' mother was a florist and her father a mortician. Her family moved to Los Angeles, and Tiegs began appearing in television commercials, where her girl-next-door looks soon brought her to the attention of local fashion photographers. At age seventeen, she appeared on the cover of *Glamour*.

In the wake of this success Tiegs set her studies aside and moved to New York City to pursue a modeling career. It was rough going for a while, but eventually Tiegs appeared on the covers of *Elle*, *Bazaar*, and *Vogue*.

With the cover shot on the 1975 *Sports Illustrated* swimsuit issue, she endeared herself to an entirely different market. The pinup poster of Tiegs scantily clad in a bikini became a best-seller, and Tiegs soon afterward signed a $1.5 million contract with Cover Girl makeup.

Tiegs published *The Way to Natural Beauty* in 1980 and endorsed her own line of casual sportswear for Sears that became wildly popular. As she approached the age of declining appeal among the young, Tiegs successfully made the transition by endorsing and designing other products, such as eyeglasses and wigs.

In November 2000 Tiegs was named the first MAC Fashion Icon, in honor of her remarkable career as an all-American girl who became America's first supermodel.

Cheryl Tiegs, the first supermodel, became the Che Guevara of her generation with a fresh and alluring *Sports Illustrated* bikini poster.

The Coen Brothers

JOEL AND ETHAN COEN grew up in St. Louis Park, and at an early age they were already collaborating on backyard Super-8 remakes of Hollywood classics. After graduating from St. Louis Park High School, the brothers went to college in the East. Ethan studied philosophy at Princeton and Joel studied film at New York University before becoming an assistant film editor for such low-budget works as *The Evil Dead* and *Fear No Evil*. In 1981 they returned to Minnesota to raise money for their own feature film, *Blood Simple*. Four years, and many trials and tribulations later, the film premiered, and it shocked the world of independent film by winning the Grand Jury Prize at the U.S. Film Festival.

As a result of this early success, the distribution rights to the Coen brothers' next film, *Raising Arizona*, which starred Nicholas Cage, Holly Hunter, and John Goodman, were bought by Twentieth Century Fox. It too, was a hit, although both audiences and critics were divided—some loved, while others hated the Coens' unusual mix of crass violence, absurdist dialogue, bizarre camera angles, and insider film references.

Undaunted by criticism, the Coens went on to win the Palme d'Or (best picture award) at the Cannes Film Festival for their 1991 film *Barton Fink*. With *Fargo* (1996), a tale of kidnapping and Scandinavian accents set in Minneapolis, they received critical acclaim on an entirely different level. The film was nominated for seven Oscars, with the brothers winning for Best Screenplay and Francis McDormand (who had recently married Joel Coen) winning for Best Supporting Actress. The American Film Institute later included the movie among the top one hundred films of all time.

The Coens continue to milk the classic genres of American filmmaking, with *The Big Lebowski* (1998), *O Brother, Where Art Thou?* (2000), *The Man Who Wasn't There* (2001), *Intolerable Cruelty* (2003), and *The Ladykillers* (2004).

Ethan (l) and Joel Coen

Undaunted by criticism, the Coen brothers won the Palme d'Or (best picture award) at the Cannes Film Festival for their 1991 film *Barton Fink*. With *Fargo* (1996), a tale of kidnapping and Scandinavian accents set in Minneapolis, they received critical acclaim on an entirely different level.

WINONA RYDER WAS BORN in Winona, Minnesota, in 1971 and lived there until she was seven years old. Her family then moved to northern California, where she lived on a hippy commune and received home schooling. As a girl Winona and her friends watched classic movies in a theater her mother set up in their barn. At age eleven she joined the American Conservatory Theater in San Francisco.

When the boyish-looking Ryder was offered a role in the movie *Lucas* (1986), she changed her last name from Horowitz to Ryder. Her breakthrough movie was *Beetlejuice* (1988), a film directed by Timothy Burton, starring Alec Baldwin, Geena Davis, and Michael Keaton. Her prominent roles in *Heathers*, *Mermaids*, *Edward Scissorhands* and *Bram Stoker's Dracula* were favorably received, and with *The Age of Innocence* (1993), Ryder ascended to the top rank of performers. She won a Golden Globe for Best Supporting Actress in this movie and was also nominated for an Oscar. Moving from strength to strength, she then starred in *Little Women* and *The Crucible* (1996). Ryder went on to roles in *Alien Resurrection* and *Celebrity*, and in 2000 she starred with Angelina Jolie in *Girl, Interrupted*. In 2002 she costarred with Adam Sandler in *Mr. Deeds*.

The actress gained a new type of notoriety when, in 2002, she was arrested in Beverley Hills on shoplifting charges. Ryder was tried and convicted of the crime and sentenced to perform community service.

Ryder briefly returned to a desirable spotlight, hosting Saturday Night Live in 2002. However, subsequent film projects such as the documentary *The Day My God Died* (2003), as well as the feature film *The Heart is Deceitful Above All Things* (2004), have not reached the mainstream.

With *The Age of Innocence* (1993), Ryder ascended to the top rank of performers. She won a Golden Globe for Best Supporting Actress in this movie and was also nominated for an Oscar.

JOEL AND ETHAN COEN

BLOOD SIMPLE

(1984) A plodding yet suspenseful thriller, it keeps your attention from start to finish.

BARTON FINK

(1991) John Turturro is a Broadway playwright who tries in vain to finish a Hollywood screenplay in this highly acclaimed yet bizarre film.

FARGO

(1996) Francis McDormand gives an Oscar-winning performance and the Coens win the Best Screenplay Oscar.

THE MAN WHO WASN'T THERE

(2001) A static but masterfully filmed crime drama, with Billy Bob Thornton as the villain.

WINONA RYDER

BEETLEJUICE

(1988) Winona Ryder plays the dry, morbid teenage daughter in this star-studded comedy.

HEATHERS

(1989) A film about high school kids, starring Ryder and Christian Slater, Heathers has become a cult classic.

BRAM STOKER'S DRACULA

(1992) Ryder plays Mina Murray/Elisabeta in the vampire movie, which received eight Oscar nominations.

THE AGE OF INNOCENCE

(1993) Ryder receives a Best Supporting Actress nomination for her portrayal of a nineteenth-century New York socialite. Also starring are Michelle Pfeifer and Daniel Day Lewis.

LITTLE WOMEN

(1994) Superbly acted by Ryder, Louisa May Alcott's Jo March comes to life as she works to become a published author during the Civil War.

Terry Gilliam

THE MULTITALENTED Terry Gilliam, well-known for his zany imagination, was born in Medicine Lake, Minnesota, in 1940. His family moved to Los Angeles when he was eleven years old. After studying political science at Occidental College, Gilliam moved to New York, where he worked as a freelance illustrator and associate editor of *HELP* magazine. His early work was heavily influenced by *Mad Magazine.*

In 1967 Gilliam moved to London to do animation for the show *Do Not Adjust Your Seat.* It was during this period that he developed his trademark cut-out style of animation, plundering old masters and old catalogs alike for striking and incongruous imagery. In 1969 he joined the troupe of the popular comedy television show *Monty Python's Flying Circus*, writing and performing in skits alongside Eric Idle, John Cleese, Michael Palin, Terry Jones, and Graham Chapman. Gilliam often provided the glue that kept the troupe functioning, and he was given complete control over his own animations.

The troupe had a successful run lampooning various aspects of modern life, but it felt the need to tackle meatier subjects. As a result, Gilliam and his cohorts began to apply their zany spirit to feature-length films, among them *Monty Python and the Holy Grail, The Meaning of Life,* (both of which Gilliam codirected), and *The Life of Brian.* Gilliam further developed his arsenal of bizarre imagery and slapstick humor in such imaginative and occasionally shocking films as *Jabberwocky, Time Bandits, Brazil,* and *The Adventures of Baron Munchausen.*

In recent times Gilliam has continued to write and direct films that expose his dreamlike and apocalyptic vision, notably *The Fisher King* and *Twelve Monkeys.* He lives in London and has been married to makeup artist Maggie Weston since 1973.

Gilliam further developed his arsenal of bizarre imagery and slapstick humor in such imaginative and occasionally shocking films as *Jabberwocky, Time Bandits, Brazil,* and *The Adventures of Baron Munchausen.*

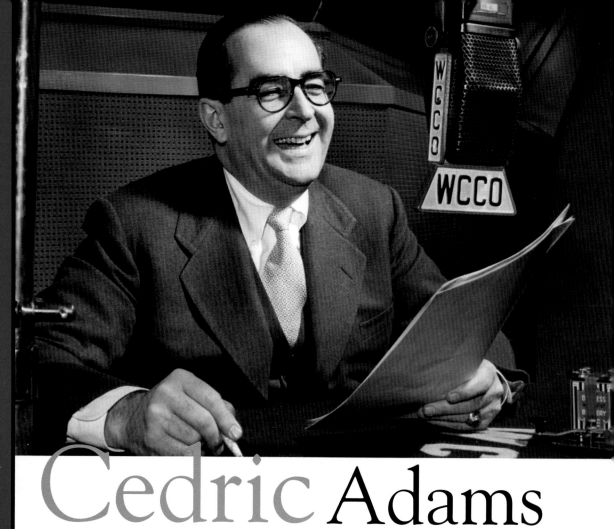

CEDRIC ADAMS

BIRTH

(1902) Cedric Adams is born on May 27, 1902, in Adrian, Minnesota.

UNIVERSITY OF MINNESOTA

(Roaring '20s) As a big man on campus, Adams majors in speech and has an English minor. He also writes for the *Minnesota Daily*, where his column "Paltry Prattle" is wildly popular.

CBS RADIO

(1949) With his corny personality Adams begins broadcasting odd facts and distinctive quips to a national audience while his sidekick, Ramona Gerhard, plays the piano or the organ. Adams would later have a five-minute Sunday program and a ten-minute series that could be heard on Monday and Tuesday nights.

CBS TELEVISION SHOWS

(1950–1951) Adams hosts talent shows on network television: *Prize Performance*, a children's talent show, and *Talent Scouts*, an Art Godfrey-hosted show with adults.

Cedric Adams

CEDRIC ADAMS WAS A POPULAR radio broadcaster who could be heard daily from coast to coast.

Adams attended Minneapolis Central High School and the University of Minnesota, where he was active on campus. The always personable Adams joined a fraternity, was a cheerleader for the Gopher football team during the playing days of the legendary Bronko Nagurski, and wrote a column in the *Minnesota Daily* called "Paltry Prattle."

In 1925 the *Minneapolis Star* newspaper asked him to write for the University section of the paper during the holidays. After the break was over Adams was offered the job full-time, but he found it difficult to fulfill the assignments while maintaining his academic workload and soon resigned.

In 1928 Adams went to work for Fawcett Publications. The company later moved to New York and Adams was out of a job. He continuing to attend classes at the University of Minnesota, while working as a salesman on the side. His radio career began in 1929, and by 1934 he was broadcasting the news for WCCO.

Eventually Adams became a national voice on CBS. His five-minute spot fell between *The Art Linkletter House Party* and *The Gary Moore Show*.

Soon Adams was being hailed by his peers as one of the best. After the advent of television he became less of a national journalist, though his popularity in Minnesota remained unsurpassed. Often referred to as the hardest working journalist in Minnesota, his day included giving the early morning radio news, then writing a newspaper column for the *Minneapolis Star Tribune*, after which he would return to the radio airwaves to broadcast the midday news. He would do the evening news on television, and complete the day with the nighttime radio news. It has been said that you could see lights going off in houses throughout the city when Adams had finished his nightly news report.

Arlene Dahl

DAHL WAS BORN ON August 11, 1928, in Minneapolis, Minnesota. Always one to have her finger in several pies, Dahl studied locally at both the University of Minnesota College of Business and the Minneapolis College of Music. At the age of twenty-one she moved to New York to pursue an acting career, and she debuted on Broadway in 1946. Before long she had made the leap to Hollywood, however, where she signed a contract with Warner Brothers, who cast her in a starring role in *My Wild Irish Rose*. A long string of similar roles with MGM followed, and Dahl soon developed a reputation as one of the most beautiful and glamorous actresses in Hollywood. Some of her best films were *Reign of Terror* (1949), *Three Little Words* (1950), *Woman's World* (1954), *Slightly Scarlet* (1956), and *Journey to the Center of the Earth* (1959).

Banking on her success on the silver screen, in 1950 Dahl began to write a beauty column, "Let's Be Beautiful," for the *Chicago Tribune / New York News Syndicate*, which ran three times a week for twenty years. While continuing her career in films, Dahl also began to market a line of beauty products and made a small fortune in the process. She was broke by the early 1980s, however, and returned to acting, appearing from 1981 to 1984 on the daytime soap opera *One Life to Live* in the role of Lucinda Schenck.

Dahl was married five times.

Dahl capitalized on her reputation as one of the most beautiful women in Hollywood to write a syndicated column and market a line of popular beauty products.

ARLENE DAHL

THREE LITTLE WORDS

(1950) An MGM film about the lives of songwriters Bert Kalmar and Harry Ruby, *Three Little Words* stars Fred Astaire as Kalmar, Red Skelton as Ruby, and Dahl as his movie star wife, Eileen Percy.

THE OUTRIDERS

(1950) Dahl is a passenger on a wagon train that's overtaken by an escaped Confederate soldier. She puts forth a memorable performance, square-dancing under the Utah sky.

BEAUTY ADVICE COLUMN

(1950-1970) Her newspaper column for the *Chicago Tribune/New York News Syndicate "Let's Be Beautiful"* is a success, appearing three days a week for twenty years.

JOURNEY TO THE CENTER OF THE EARTH

(1959) Also starring James Mason and Pat Boone, *Journey* is about a group of explorers with Dahl playing the widow of a renowned geologist.

ONE LIFE TO LIVE

(1981–1984) Dahl returns to the limelight in the role of Lucinda Schenk on the popular daytime drama about people in a Pennsylvania town.

EDDIE ALBERT

ROMAN HOLIDAY

(1953) Eddie Albert is Irving Radovich, a photographer with an American correspondent (Gregory Peck) in Rome. The two of them meet Princess Anne (Audrey Hepburn), and Albert tries to snap a photo of her. The movie received thirteen Academy Award nominations. Albert was nominated for Best Supporting Actor.

I'LL CRY TOMORROW

(1955) Albert stars opposite Susan Hayward in this film, which is based on the real life of singer Lillian Roth.

THE LONGEST DAY

(1962) In this movie about the Normandy invasion, Albert stars with John Wayne, Henry Fonda, and Robert Mitchum. The film receives twelve Academy Award nominations.

THE HEARTBREAK KID

(1972) Albert receives a Best Supporting Actor nomination for his portrayal of a curmudgeon who opposes his daughter's marriage. Neil Simon wrote the script and Elaine May directed.

THE LONGEST YARD

(1974) As the warden of a Georgia prison, a stern Albert tries to predetermine the outcome of an upcoming football game between the guards and inmates, the latter of which is led by a tough quarterback (Burt Reynolds).

EDDIE ALBERT WAS NOMINATED for Best Supporting Actor for his roles in the movies *Roman Holiday* (1953) and *The Heartbreak Kid* (1972), but it was in the role of Oliver on the popular 1960s television sitcom *Green Acres* that Albert gained widespread popularity.

Albert's real name was Heimberger. He was raised in Minneapolis. After attending the University of Minnesota, Albert moved to New York, where he performed in the circus, on radio, and in the theater. In 1936 he became a television pioneer, starring in the first experimental NBC telecast. Soon afterward he scored a hit on stage in the role of Bing Edwards in *Brother Rat*. Two years later he moved to Hollywood to reprise the role on film.

During World War II, Albert distinguished himself at the Battle of Tawara, earning a Bronze Star for his bravery under fire. Sent ashore to examine military equipment for possible salvage, Arnold chose instead to save the wounded Marines lying on the beach and became a war hero.

Albert went on to become a major film star, appearing in more than fifty movies. He was known for supporting comedy roles in *Roman Holiday* and other films, but he displayed the full range of his talents in films like *The Longest Day* and *Attack!!*, where he plays a cowardly army officer.

Albert's career took another turn when he happened to notice that the pelicans near his Southern California home weren't reproducing. Stirred to investigate the mystery, he eventually went on a speaking tour of over sixty colleges and universities, urging that the pesticide DDT be banned. In honor of his early efforts on behalf of environmental causes, Albert's birthday, April 22, was chosen to commemorate Earth Day.

A long-time resident of Pacific Palisades in Los Angeles, California, Albert died in 2005, at the age of 99. Three days before his death he was seen playing basketball in a wheelchair with his granddaughter.

Robert
Vaughn

THE SON OF TWO professional actors, Robert Vaughn began his career as a child radio performer. Originally from New York, Vaughn attended Minneapolis North High School, where he was a standout trackman and received a scholarship from the University of Minnesota. He spent some time as a sports reporter for the *Minneapolis Star-Journal*, and also worked at a local radio station before moving with his family to California in the mid-1950s.

After completing his undergraduate degree and serving in the military, Vaughn returned to acting and in 1959 received an Oscar nomination for Best Supporting Actor for his portrayal of a one-armed drunk in *The Young Philadelphians*. He also figured prominently in *The Magnificent Seven* and *Bullitt*, but it was his portrayal of Napoleon Solo, the suave undercover agent, in the 1960s television shows *The Man from U.N.C.L.E.*, that remains Vaughn's greatest claim to fame.

Meanwhile, Vaughn continued his education, receiving his MA and PhD degrees in political science from UCLA. He has held leadership roles in the Democratic Party of Southern California, while continuing to work sporadically in films and television. He recently appeared on three episodes of *Law and Order*, and in the movie *Pootie Tang* (2001).

RICHARD DEAN ANDERSON was the intellectual action hero on the nighttime television show *MacGyver*. Premiering in 1985, it ran for seven seasons.

Anderson grew up in Roseville in the midst of an artistic family, but his personal dream was to become a professional hockey player. He broke both arms while playing hockey, however, and turned his attention to less violent pursuits. His love of adventure remained avid, however, and at the age of seventeen he rode his bicycle from Minnesota to Alaska, a distance of more than 5,000 miles.

Anderson studied acting in college and spent several years as a struggling performer in Los Angeles, where he found work as a juggler and performer in marine animal shows. From these modest beginnings he landed a few roles in theater, and in 1976 he was cast as Dr. Jeff Webber on the soap opera *General Hospital*.

During the early 1980s Anderson appeared on various nighttime shows, including *The Facts of Life*, *Seven Brides for Seven Brothers*, and *Emerald Point N.A.S.* It was with the role of *MacGyver*, however, that he came to enjoy widespread popularity. *MacGyver* was on the air for seven seasons, during which time the unpretentious hero met a variety of challenges making use of ingenuity and whatever materials lay close at hand. Anderson later appeared in several *MacGyver* films, before setting out on a second successful series with *Stargate SG-1*, in which he leads a group of experts on missions here and there throughout several universes.

Anderson grew up in Roseville with dreams of becoming a professional hockey player. Instead of hockey he went into show business.

Richard Dean Anderson

Richard Widmark

WIDMARK WAS BORN ON December 26, 1914, in Sunrise, Minnesota. The son of a traveling salesman, he lived in several midwestern communities during his youth, before heading to the Chicago area to study law at Lake Forest College. At Lake Forest Widmark took a liking to the theater, however, and he taught briefly in the drama department there before moving to New York City to become an actor.

Widmark became a popular radio personality in New York, starring on the daytime soap opera *Front Page Farrell* from 1938 to 1947. He also starred in several Broadway productions before leaving for Hollywood. His first film role, as the creepy mobster Tommy Udo in the major motion picture *Kiss of Death* (1947), brought him instant celebrity and an Academy Award nomination for Best Supporting Actor.

Widmark went on to appear in more than forty films, including *Panic in the Streets* (1950), *The Alamo* (1961), *Judgment at Nuremberg* (1961), *Madigan* (1968), *Murder on the Orient Express* (1974), *A Gathering of Old Men* (1987), and *True Colors* (1991).

Loni Anderson

LONI ANDERSON BECAME well known when she starred in the hit sitcom *WKRP in Cincinnati*. Before that time she had appeared in various TV series, including *The Bob Newhart Show*, *Three's Company*, and *The Incredible Hulk*.

Anderson was born in St. Paul in 1945, raised in Roseville, and graduated from Alexander Ramsey High School. In 1963 she was named Miss Roseville and in 1964 was first runner-up for Miss Minnesota.

She attended the University of Minnesota, where she received a B.A. in art. At that time she also appeared in local theater productions.

Following her success in *WKRP* she appeared in TV movies, including the successful *Jane Mansfield Story*. Her most recent work was as a regular on the short-lived TV show *The Mullets*.

Warren Burger

WARREN BURGER, WHO WOULD one day become the fifteenth chief justice of the U.S. Supreme Court, was born in St. Paul, Minnesota, on September 17, 1907. The son of a railroad cargo inspector, he graduated from the St. Paul College of Law in 1931 and went into private practice, while also teaching courses in contract law at his alma mater (since renamed William Mitchell College of Law).

Burger was a staunch Republican and became floor manager at the 1948 and 1952 Republican conventions. In 1955, President Dwight D. Eisenhower appointed him to the U.S. Court of Appeals for the District of Columbia. During his tenure on that bench Burger developed a reputation for supporting the activities of prosecutors against suspected criminals, and as a result, in 1969 President Richard M. Nixon, who had campaigned on a law-and-order platform, nominated Burger as Chief Justice to the Supreme Court.

Nixon's hope was that Burger would stem the liberal tide of the Warren Court, and in this he was not entirely disappointed. Burger was not a great jurist, however, and he found himself in the minority on many key issues, including affirmative action and the release of the Pentagon Papers. Too liberal for many conservatives, and far too conservative for most liberals, Burger, by the time he retired in 1986 as the century's longest-serving chief justice, had come to be viewed as vacillating in the sea-change between the liberal 1960s and the more conservative times that followed. And yet, ironically, Burger took a strong stand in what is perhaps his most famous case. In *United States v. Nixon* (1974) Burger ordered the president who had appointed him to turn over the Watergate Tapes to special prosecutor Leon Jaworski, a ruling that led directly to the president's resignation.

Too liberal for many conservatives, and far too conservative for most liberals, Burger, by the time he retired in 1986 as the century's longest-serving chief justice, had come to be viewed as vacillating in the sea-change between the liberal 1960s and the more conservative times that followed.

W. HARRY DAVIS

W. Harry Davis

W. HARRY DAVIS, A LEADING advocate of civil rights in Minneapolis for most of his life, is perhaps best remembered as the first African American to win major-party endorsement for mayor of Minneapolis.

His mayoral campaign in 1971 was not successful. But Davis was elected handily to the city's school board in 1969 and served 20 years, leading the city's schools through court-ordered desegregation and the significant downsizing of the 1980s.

School desegregation and optional busing were central issues in his mayoral contest with incumbent Charlie Stenvig, an integration opponent. The campaign was heated, coming on the heels of serious racial tension in the city in the mid-1960s. During the campaign, Davis received repeated death threats and was under protective guard around the clock.

Davis was also the founding executive director of the Urban Coalition of Minneapolis, head of the Hennepin County War on Poverty program, and an executive at the *Star Tribune* newspaper for 14 years. He was instrumental in bringing about a groundbreaking merger of his all-black Methodist congregation with an all-white congregation in the 1950s.

In addition, he was the most successful Golden Gloves boxing coach in the Upper Midwest in the 1950s and an administrator of youth boxing programs for two decades. In the 1980s, he was a member of the U.S. Olympic Boxing Committee, and was one of the managers of the 1984 U.S. Olympic boxing team.

Born in North Minneapolis in 1923, Davis has lived all his life in the city. He and his late wife, Charlotte Napue Davis, have four children.

Roy Wilkins

ROY WILKINS WAS BORN in St. Louis, Missouri, in 1901. His mother died when he was five, and Roy was sent to live with relatives in St. Paul. He attended Mechanic Arts High School and then the University of Minnesota, with hopes of becoming an engineer, but later decided to focus on sociology and journalism. During his student years Wilkins was a reporter and editor at the campus newspaper, *The Minnesota Daily*, and a reporter for *Appeal*, a black weekly paper in St. Paul.

Upon graduation in 1923 Wilkins moved to Kansas City, Missouri, to join the staff of *The Call*, a black weekly newspaper. In Kansas City he met and fell in love with a social worker from St. Louis named Aminda Badeau. His work came to the attention of Walter White, at that time executive secretary of the National Association for the Advancement of Colored People (NAACP), and in 1931 Wilkins moved to New York to become White's assistant. In that capacity he edited the organization's official magazine, *Crisis*, and wrote exposés on racist practices, including lynching, that were then common in the South.

In 1955 Wilkins became executive director of the NAACP. As the civil rights movement gathered steam, he became an effective spokesman for nonviolent change, conferring with presidents from John F. Kennedy to Jimmy Carter. Although his reliance on legislation and the court system was deemed to be outmoded and ineffective by the leaders of more militant civil rights groups, under Wilkins's leadership the NAACP quietly provided invaluable assistance to many ghetto communities in northern cities, while tirelessly working to establish the legal foundations for fair housing, equal opportunity in employment, and integration.

Wilkins retired from the NAACP in 1977. He published his autobiography, *Standing Fast,* in 1982.

Hubert Humphrey

HUBERT H. HUMPHREY was born on May 27, 1911, in Wallace, South Dakota. The son of a pharmacist, Humphrey was trained as a pharmacist himself, and worked in the family business for several years before completing a degree at the University of Minnesota in 1939. He went on to earn an advanced degree in political science, and was soon deeply involved in state politics, eventually becoming mayor of Minneapolis. While he was mayor Humphrey facilitated the enactment of fair employment practices in the city, and at the 1948 Democratic National Convention he made a stirring speech in defense of the minority position on civil rights that effectively transformed the convention. Humphrey went on to serve six terms in the U.S. Senate, during which time issues of human rights remained in the forefront of his political agenda.

Humphrey was instrumental in enacting the Civil Rights Act in 1964 and Medicare legislation in 1965.

Active with international politics as well, he was on the Senate Foreign Relations Committee, was chairman of the Middle East Subcommittee on Foreign Relations, and was a delegate to the General Assembly of the United Nations.

Humphrey's career changed radically, however, when President Lyndon Johnson chose him as a running mate in 1964. As vice president Humphrey had greater prominence than ever, but less impact on policy and legislation, and his loyalty to the Johnson administration hobbled his efforts to chart a new course in Southeast Asia following Johnson's decision not to seek reelection.

In 1968, after a fierce struggle, Humphrey won the Democratic nomination for president but lost the general election by a narrow margin to the Republican Party candidate Richard Nixon. He returned to the U.S. Senate in 1970, and served as the majority whip until his death from cancer in 1978.

Humphrey served six terms in the U.S. Senate, during which time issues of human rights remained in the forefront of his political agenda.

THE SON OF AN ARMY OFFICER, Colby was born in St. Paul on January 4, 1920. He attended Princeton University, graduating with a bachelor's degree in 1940. During World War II Colby worked in the Office of Strategic Services—the forerunner of the CIA—and engaged in covert operations behind enemy lines in both France and Norway. After the war he returned to college, received a law degree from Columbia University, and set up in private practice, but he found the work too dull and joined the newly created CIA.

During the 1950s Colby was the U.S. embassy attaché in Stockholm, Sweden, the special assistant to the U.S. embassy in Rome, and the first secretary assigned to Saigon. In 1962 Colby returned to Washington to become chief of the CIA's Far East division, where he was responsible for monitoring American activities in Vietnam.

In 1968 Colby returned to Saigon to administer a controversial "pacification" program called Operation Phoenix. Called on the carpet by the Senate Foreign Relations Committee in 1971, he returned to covert operations, and in May 1973 Richard Nixon nominated him to head the CIA.

Colby's tenure as head of the CIA is considered by many to be the most controversial in its short history, largely because he took the unusual step of revealing to Congress all of the CIA operations that were in violation of its charter. Critics inside the agency felt that he had revealed far too much about its operations—his view was that Congress would find these things out anyway, and it was better if the agency controlled how the story was told. It was also interesting to note that nearly all of the illegal activities had been by explicit presidential request.

Colby was fired from the agency in 1975, and returned to private practice. In later life he campaigned against the nuclear arms race, founded an organization for the development of a democratic Vietnam, and wrote two books: *Honorable Men: My Life in the CIA*, published in 1978; and *Lost Victory*, published in 1989.

William Colby

Harry Blackmun

HARRY BLACKMUN WAS the U.S. Supreme Court justice who wrote the decision in *Roe v. Wade*, the landmark case that legalized abortion in the United States.

Born in Nashville, Illinois, in 1908, Blackmun grew up in St. Paul and attended Mechanic Arts High School. Though he received a scholarship to attend Harvard University, he also worked as a janitor, a milkman, and a paper-grader to make ends meet during those years—experiences that contributed to his lifelong conviction that the study and application of law is inseparable from its effect on ordinary people.

After graduation from Harvard Law School, Blackmun returned to Minnesota and was admitted to the bar in 1934. He joined the firm of Dorsey, Colman, Barker, Scott, and Barber as an associate. Nine years later he became general partner at the firm. The Mayo Clinic hired him in 1950 as its resident council. Nine years later, President Dwight D. Eisenhower appointed him to the U.S. Court of Appeals, Eighth Circuit.

In 1970 President Richard M. Nixon nominated Blackmun to the Supreme Court and the Senate confirmed him. In his early years on the bench Blackmun often defended establishment positions, but with time his concern for individual rights came to figure more prominently in his decisions. Perhaps his most controversial ruling, and certainly the one for which he is best known, was the 1973 *Roe v. Wade* decision, which affirmed a woman's right to have an abortion.

In his final years, as the court shifted to the right, Blackmun became a moderating force in upholding affirmative action, the separation of church and state, and the rights of immigrants and minorities. He retired in 1994 at the age of 85. He died in 1999.

HARRY BLACKMUN

BIRTHPLACE

(1908) Harry Blackmun is born in Nashville, Illinois.

ST. PAUL

(1925) In the shadows of the state capitol building Blackmun graduates from Mechanic Arts High School.

HARVARD

(1925–1932) Blackmun obtains degrees in mathematics and law from the prestigious school.

MINNESOTA BAR

(1934) He is admitted to the Minnesota Bar and joins the firm of Dorsey, Colman, Barker, Scott and Barber.

ROE V. WADE

(1973) Blackmun authors a lengthy majority opinion for the U.S. Supreme Court, siding with Roe in her case in defense of abortion rights.

Elmer Andersen

ELMER L. ANDERSEN was the thirtieth governor of Minnesota, serving from 1961 to 1963.

Upon graduating from the University of Minnesota in 1931, Andersen went to work for H. B. Fuller Company. By 1941, he was president and chairman of the board of the corporation. His political career began to take shape in 1948 when he was elected to the Minnesota State Senate. Andersen was a state senator for ten years before stepping down in 1959. He campaigned for governor and was elected on the Republican ticket. During his time as governor, Andersen worked to establish a withholding system for state income tax and to pass legislation to ensure fair housing and equal employment opportunities for minorities. He was also instrumental in improving the state education system.

Following his single term as governor, Andersen returned to H. B. Fuller, but his contributions to the civic and community life of the state continued.

Among the many projects he supported were the establishment of Southwest University and the founding of Voyageur National Park. Andersen served for many years on the Board of Regents at the University of Minnesota, and his involvement in philanthropic organizations, among them the Elmer L. and Eleanor J. Andersen Foundation, has been unparalleled. In recognition of his many contributions to the educational and cultural life of the state, the University of Minnesota named their new library in his honor, and the State of Minnesota, in recognition of his efforts on behalf of adoption agencies, the mentally ill, and the disabled, funded the Elmer L. Andersen Human Services Building.

Andersen retells his colorful and inspiring life story in *A Man's Reach*. The political and social insights that have given him the aura of a true elder statesman can be found in the book *I Trust to be Believed: Speeches and Reflections*.

Gus Hall

GUS HALL, THE SON OF Finnish immigrants, was born Arvo Gus Halberg on October 8, 1910. His parents were deeply involved in the Industrial Workers of the World, a syndicalist labor organization, and became charter members of the Communist Party in 1919. Hall followed in their footsteps, studying for two years at the Lenin Institute in Moscow and participating in the famous Minneapolis Teamsters' strike of 1934. He later led a steelworkers strike in Youngstown, Ohio, and ran for mayor of Youngstown on the Communist ticket.

Hall served in the navy during World War II, but after the war he returned to his left-wing political activities and was indicted under the Smith Act in 1948. He fled to Mexico but was apprehended by the authorities and spent the next few years in prison.

Upon his release from Leavenworth Prison in 1957, Hall, an unreconstructed Stalinist (Stalin himself had died in 1953)

entered into a bitter struggle with John Gates, editor of the *Daily Worker*, to shape the future of the Communist Party, at a time when workers were already leaving it in droves. Eventually Hall became the general secretary of the U.S. branch of the party, and he ran for president in 1968 alongside fellow-Minnesotans Eugene McCarthy, Hubert Humphrey, and Harold Stassen, but Hall received only 1,075 votes. Hall threw his hat into the ring on several more occasions, though he had no chance of winning, and in 1984 he finally desisted from his quixotic quest to lead the country and gave his support to Democratic candidate Jesse Jackson.

Hall continued to lead the U.S. Communist Party until his death in 2000, though his presence on the political scene was negligible. In later life Hall also turned to the pen to advance his cause, publishing *The Energy Rip-Off* (1974), *Working Class USA: The Power and the Movement* (1987), and several other titles.

Hall became the general secretary of the American branch of the Communist Party, and he ran for president in 1968 alongside fellow-Minnesotans Eugene McCarthy, Hubert Humphrey, and Harold Stassen, but received only 1,075 votes.

BORN

Wellstone was born on July 21, 1944, the son of Russian Jewish immigrants.

MARRIAGE

(1963) Wellstone marries Shiela Ison, who advises, supports and contributes to his political activities, while eventually developing her own reputation as an advocate for battered women.

POWER-LINE DISPUTE

(2000) Wellstone lends his grass-roots organizational skills to farmers in western Minnesota who are opposed to the construction of high-powered lines across their fields.

GREEN BUS

(1990) During his first campaign for U.S. Senate, Wellstone captures the attention of voters by crisscrossing the state in a dilapidated green school bus.

EUGENE MCCARTHY

BIRTHPLACE

(1916) Eugene McCarthy is born in Watkins, Minnesota.

COLLEGE PROFESSOR

(1946–1949) Taught economics and sociology at St. Thomas College.

CONGRESSMAN MCCARTHY

(1949–1959) The liberal Democrat represents Minnesota's Fourth Congressional District.

SENATOR MCCARTHY

(1959–1970) The newly elected senator joins Hubert Humphrey in Washington.

PRESIDENTIAL CANDIDATE

(1968) A strong showing by McCarthy in the New Hampshire primary contributes to President Johnson's decision not to seek reelection. McCarthy would not be nominated, however. Democratic convention delegates choose Hubert Humphrey instead.

Paul Wellstone

PAUL WELLSTONE, THE OUTSPOKEN senator, was born and raised in the Washington D.C. area. A championship wrestler, he studied political science at the University of North Carolina, receiving his Ph.D. in 1969. For the next twenty years Wellstone applied his scrappy approach to scholarship and social issues at Carleton College in Northfield, Minnesota, where he was hired as a professor of political science. He encouraged his students to become involved in local politics and to speak out forcefully against injustice. Wellstone himself became involved as an organizer in a rural power-line dispute, and he entered the larger political arena by running for state auditor in 1982.

A defeat in that election did nothing to dampen Wellstone's growing enthusiasm for public life, and in 1990 he took on popular Republican senator Rudy Boschwitz, running an underfunded but energetic campaign as a "people's" candidate that eventually brought Boschwitz down.

Once in the Senate, Wellstone found it expedient to temper his fiery and outspoken style, yet he never altered his vision for the future of the country, or his concern that the interests of common people were under-represented in the halls of state. He consistently opposed President Clinton's centrist solutions to social problems and seriously explored the possibility of running for president in the 2000 elections. He worked in the Senate for sensible energy policy, for extending medical benefits to cover mental illness, and on behalf of veterans. He was the only Democrat facing reelection in 2002 to oppose the bill granting President Bush the power to act unilaterally in Iraq.

Wellstone and his wife Sheila, their daughter Marcia, and three staff aids were killed in a plane crash on October 25, 2002, on the eve of elections for his third term in office.

Considered in retrospect, Wellstone's specific contributions to public life as a legislator, though significant, are perhaps surpassed by the shining example he offered of a true public servant. The specifics of his vision for the future of American democracy are detailed in his book, aptly titled *The Conscience of a Liberal.*

EUGENE MCCARTHY WAS BORN on March 29, 1916, in Watkins, Minnesota. As a youth he became a novitiate at St. John's Benedictine Abbey in Collegeville, Minnesota, but later withdrew from the order and received his bachelor's degree in 1935 from St. John's University. Three years later he earned his master's degree from the University of Minnesota. He taught economics at St. John's for two years, and served as a military intelligence technician during World War II. Following the war McCarthy returned to teaching at the College of St. Thomas, where he eventually became the head of the sociology department.

In 1947 McCarthy rose to political prominence as chairman of the newly formed Democratic Farm Labor Party in Ramsey County. He was elected to U.S. Congress in 1948, representing the Fourth District of Minnesota, and focused his attention on unemployment and personal privacy issues. His reputation for both integrity and controversy was heightened when he courageously debated Senator Joe McCarthy on national television. After four terms in the House, McCarthy was elected to the U.S. Senate in 1958.

McCarthy gained considerable power and influence in Washington in 1965, when he was appointed to the Senate Foreign Relations Committee. An outspoken critic of the government's policies in Southeast Asia, he campaigned for the Democratic nomination for president in 1968 against incumbent and fellow Democrat Lyndon Johnson. McCarthy fared surprisingly well, though he didn't win in the New Hampshire primary. This shocking result brought about President Johnson's decision to withdraw from the race, opening the field for McCarthy and other high-profile challengers including New York Senator Robert Kennedy, Vice President Hubert Humphrey, and Maine Senator Edmund Muskie. Kennedy won the California primary, yet later that night he was assassinated. For the remainder of the long, hot summer the candidates voiced their opinions and answered questions. McCarthy was clearly against the Vietnam War.

Since then McCarthy has written several books and continues to make thoughtful and idiosyncratic pronouncements on a variety of issues.

Eugene McCarthy

Harold Stassen

HAROLD STASSEN WAS A MEMBER of the U.S. delegation to the original United Nations Charter meetings in 1945. He was also a frequent presidential candidate. One of his favorite remarks in later life was, "I tried."

Born on April 13, 1907, in Dakota County, Stassen graduated from Humboldt High School in St. Paul at the age of fifteen. He attended the University of Minnesota Law School, after which he was admitted to the Minnesota Bar at the tender age of twenty-one. He was elected Dakota County attorney at age twenty-three.

Stassen, a Republican, was elected governor of Minnesota in 1938 at the age of thirty-one—the youngest from any state to have held that office—and he was re-elected in 1940 and 1942. The wonder boy gave the keynote address at the Republican National Convention in 1940, and he might have been drafted to run against Franklin Delano Roosevelt except that he was too young at the time to become president.

Stassen resigned from his governorship in 1943 to join the navy, serving as an aide to Admiral William T. Halsey, the commander of the Third Fleet in the Pacific. After the war Stassen was involved in helping draft the United Nations Charter.

In 1948, Stassen lost the Republican presidential nomination to Thomas Dewey, who ran a lackluster campaign and lost to Harry Truman in the general election. Stassen threw his hat back in the ring in 1952, only to come face to face with the wildly popular General Dwight D. Eisenhower at the Republican National Convention.

After winning the presidential election that year, Eisenhower appointed Stassen director of his foreign aid operations. Stassen was also a member of the National Security Council from 1953 to 1958 and an advisor on disarmament, but his criticisms of Vice President Richard Nixon, and his involvement with the United Nations, which Republicans tended to view with suspicion, drove many in the party to label him as a liberal who would be better off with the Democrats.

Stassen returned to Minnesota in 1978 to practice law, but he continued to seek the post that had eluded him during his glory years in Washington. He was a perennial, if quixotic, presidential candidate, running in 1964, 1968, 1976, 1980, 1984, 1988, and 1992. Stassen died on March 4, 2001.

Frank B. Kellogg

FRANK B. KELLOGG was born December 22, 1856, in Potsdam, New York. His family headed west when he was nine, settling in Elgin, Minnesota. Kellogg attended a country school, and worked on the family farm for five years before making his escape to nearby Rochester, where he took a job as a clerk in a law office—for no pay—and worked as a handyman to support himself. Struggling to overcome the deficiencies of a spotty primary education, Kellogg also found time to study history, Latin, German, and law on his own, and within two years he had passed the Minnesota Bar exam.

Not long afterward Kellogg formed a law practice with another attorney, and in 1886, at the age of thirty-five, Kellogg won the election for the office of district attorney. But his true rise to prominence only began when his work on a difficult case brought him to the attention of Cushman K. Davis, Minnesota's leading lawyer at the time. Once he'd joined Cushman's firm, contacts with railroad and mining barons soon followed, and Kellogg could leave his humble beginnings behind forever. Ironically, Kellogg first came to national prominence as a result of cases against railroad financier Edward H. Harri-man and the Standard Oil Trust.

In 1912 Kellogg was elected to the U.S. Senate. He lost his seat in 1916, and also failed in a re-election bid in 1922, but was appointed ambassador to Great Britain, and later secretary of state by President Calvin Coolidge. It was in this capacity that Kellogg played a central role in the 1928 Pact of Paris, also known as the Kellogg-Briand Pact.

This treaty, which renounced war as an instrument of national policy, began as the brain-child of the French foreign minister Briand, who imagined a bi-lateral agreement between France and the United States. Kellogg broadened the base of the treaty to include anyone willing to come on board, and it was eventually signed by sixty-two nations. As a result of this historic, if ultimately ineffective, treaty, Kellogg was awarded the Nobel Peace Prize the following year. He was appointed to the Permanent Court of International Justice at The Hague in the same year, and was later elected to the same seat.

In 1937, Kellogg donated $500,000 to Carlton College in Northfield, Minnesota, for an international relations study program. He died later that year.

Kellogg played a central role in the 1928 Pact of Paris, also known as the Kellogg-Briand Pact. This treaty, which renounced war as an instrument of national policy, began as the brain-child of the French foreign minister Briand. As a result of this historic, if ultimately ineffective, treaty, Kellogg was awarded the Nobel Peace Prize the following year.

HAROLD STASSEN

HIGH SCHOOL
(1922) Stassen graduates from Humboldt High School at the tender age of fifteen.

PROSECUTOR
(1930) Stassen is elected Dakota County prosecutor at the age of twenty-three.

GOVERNOR
(1938) He begins his first term as governor of Minnesota at age thirty-one, becoming the youngest ever to hold that office. He would successfully run for reelection in 1940.

THE ELUSIVE PRESIDENCY
(1948) Stassen runs for the Republican nomination for president but loses out to Thomas Dewey. He would run again and again, but to no avail, for more than forty years.

FRANK KELLOGG

BIRTHPLACE
(1856) Frank Kellogg is born in Potsdam, New York.

MINNESOTA
(1865–1870) As a farm boy living in Elgin, Kellogg attends a country school.

BAR EXAM
(1877) After years of teaching himself by reading books, Kellogg passes the Minnesota Bar Exam.

SENATOR KELLOGG
(1916) Kellogg, who had been a delegate at the Republican National Conventions in 1904, 1908, and 1912, runs for office and is elected to the U.S. Senate.

NOBEL PRIZE
(1929) As secretary of state under President Calvin Coolidge, Kellogg negotiates the Pact of Paris, renouncing war as an instrument of national policy. For this he is awarded the Nobel Peace Prize.

Walter Mondale

FORMER VICE PRESIDENT Walter Mondale was born in Ceylon, Minnesota, in 1928. He graduated from the University of Minnesota in 1951 and gained his early political experience working on the campaign of Minneapolis mayor Hubert Humphrey.

Mondale served in the army during the Korean War but remained stateside. He eventually earned his law degree from the University of Minnesota and began practicing law.

In 1960, Mondale worked on the reelection campaign of Minnesota governor Orville Freeman. Later that year Mondale accepted Freeman's appointment as Minnesota state attorney general. He was elected to the office in 1962 and appointed to the U.S. Senate in 1964 by Governor Karl Rølvaag.

A few of the controversial programs Mondale backed during his thirteen years as a senator were open housing, busing students for school integration, education for American Indians, and tax reform. He was Jimmy Carter's running mate in the 1976 presidential election. They were successful in their bid for the White House, defeating incumbent Gerald Ford and his running mate Robert Dole.

One of the duo's biggest achievements while in office was the signing of the Camp David Peace Accord between Israel and Palestine. In 1980, Carter and Mondale ran for reelection but were defeated by Republicans Ronald Reagan and George Bush.

In 1984, Mondale received the Democratic nomination for president. In a bold move, he chose a woman, Geraldine Ferraro, as his running mate. After catching Ronald Reagan off guard in their first debate, Mondale lost ground and was soundly defeated by Reagan in the second debate and in the November election. Since then Mondale has continued practicing law, is a consultant on the boards of several large corporations, and served as the U.S. ambassador to Japan from 1993 to 1997.

Mondale returned to political life briefly in the fall of 2002, when he ran for U.S. Senate in the place of incumbent Senator Paul Wellstone, who had been killed in a plane crash eleven days before the November election. Mondale lost the crucial election by a narrow margin to Norm Coleman.

Mondale married the former Joan Adams in 1955. They have a daughter and two sons.

A few of the controversial programs Mondale backed during his thirteen years as a senator were open housing, busing students for school integration, education for American Indians, and tax reform.

45

KEVIN GARNETT

TIMBERWOLVES DRAFT THE KID

(1995) A franchise with a woeful past, the Timberwolves are in dire need of an impact player and find one in the versatile, sleek, seven-foot forward named Kevin Garnett.

LOOKING TO THE FUTURE

(1997) Considered by *Newsweek* magazine to be one of the most influential people of the next decade, Garnett makes Wolves owner Glen Taylor proud.

GARNETT TAKES OVER

(2000) Garnett, a dominating shooter, replaces journeyman Sam Mitchell as the team's all-time points leader.

IN THE STARTING LINEUP

(2002–2003) He is a starter in all eighty-two games of the grueling NBA regular season.

THIS ONE'S FOR KEEPS

(2003–2004) In the second round of the NBA play-off series against the Sacramento Kings, Garnett does it all and successfully defends a three-point attempt by Chris Weber, ending game seven.

THE ATHLETES

Kevin Garnett

IN 1995 KEVIN GARNETT was drafted by the Minnesota Timberwolves of the National Basketball Association (NBA), becoming the first high school player to be drafted since Moses Malone was selected by the Utah Jazz of the American Basketball Association in 1974.

Garnett was born on May 19, 1976, in Mauldin, South Carolina. He attended high school in Mauldin, but moved to Chicago, Illinois, played for Farragut Academy, and was named the most outstanding high school player in the nation by *USA Today*. The Minnesota Timberwolves selected Garnett in the first round of the 1995 NBA draft with the fifth overall pick. Garnett made the NBA All-Rookie Second Team in 1996. The Timberwolves, who had not had success with many of their first round draft picks, finally made a great choice in Garnett. He gave the Wolves a new image. The team, which had struggled for fifteen years, now had a future. The Wolves made the play-offs for the first time in 1997. They continued to make the play-offs, although they did not win a first round series for seven consecutive seasons. Garnett, however, became one of the most dominant players in the NBA, and in 2004, he was named the Most Valuable Player. Meanwhile, the Timberwolves won their first Midwest Division Championship. They won their first play-off series, beating the Denver Nuggets. From there they went on to defeat the Sacramento Kings in seven games before losing to the Los Angeles Lakers in the conference finals. Garnett's season was truly one for the ages.

During the 2004-2005 season the Timberwolves had high hopes, but they failed even to make the play-offs, though Garnett himself led the league in rebounds and once again performed at the highest level.

He has made Minnesota his home.

Kevin Garnett has become one of the most dominant players in the NBA, and in 2004 he was named the Most Valuable Player.

ONE OF THE GREATEST sports announcements in Minnesota history was sportscaster Jack Buck's "We will see you tomorrow night" after Kirby Puckett hit the winning homer in game six of the 1991 World Series.

Born on March 14, 1960, in Chicago, Illinois, Puckett was the youngest of nine children. He grew up in the Taylor housing project in South Chicago, but he later moved out of the project and attended Calumet High School. He later worked on an assembly line for Ford Motor Company to pay the bills and played ball whenever he could.

Puckett accepted a scholarship to Bradley University, but after the untimely death of his father, he returned home to attend Triton Community College, where his talents caught the eye of Twins' scout Jim Rantz. The Twins made him the third pick of the 1982 draft, and after finishing up the season at Triton he signed a minor league contract.

Puckett toiled in the minor leagues for two seasons before joining the Twins in 1984, but from the beginning his enthusiasm was rampant. When he hit a ground ball, he hustled down the first base line as fast as he could. He carried this joyful, carefree attitude into the outfield as well, and in time Puckett became the top center fielder in baseball. He often scaled the walls of American League stadiums, robbing players of home runs, including Ron Grant of the Atlanta Braves in game six of the 1991 World Series.

Puckett's career was cut short by an eye injury he suffered at the plate in 1995. Some of the more noteworthy accomplishments of his abbreviated career are six Gold Gloves, ten all-star game appearances, 2,000 hits faster than any player in the history of the game, and World Series championships in 1987 and 1991.

Puckett won both the Branch Rickey Award (1993) and the Roberto Clemente Man of the Year Award (1996) for his community service. Puckett was inducted into the National Baseball Hall of Fame on the first ballot in 2001.

From the beginning Puckett's enthusiasm was rampant. When he hit a ground ball, he hustled down the first base line as fast as he could. He carried this joyful, carefree attitude into the outfield as well, and in time Puckett became the top center fielder in baseball.

Kirby Puckett

Paul Molitor

PAUL MOLITOR'S TOWERING stature as a baseball player may be suggested by the fact that in 1997 the Baseball Writers of America selected him as the designated hitter on their major league baseball all-time team, an honor that placed him in the company of Babe Ruth (right fielder), Johnny Bench (catcher), and Mike Schmidt (third baseman).

Molitor rose to local prominence playing ball at St. Paul's Cretin High School, and he was later voted All American for his play with the University of Minnesota Golden Gophers.

He began his professional career with the Milwaukee Brewers. During the next twenty-one seasons he played with the Brewers, the Toronto Blue Jays, and the Minnesota Twins, compiling numbers that put him among the top twenty players in the history of the sport in several categories, including at bats, hits, runs, singles, doubles, triples, and stolen bases. In particular, his 3,319 hits place him eighth of all time. Explosive at the plate and aggressive on the base paths, Molitor was also steady in the field, and he played nearly every position at one time or another.

Some of the memorable achievements during his illustrious career were American League Rookie of the Year in 1978, Most Valuable Player of the 1993 World Series, and his 3,000th hit as a member of the Minnesota Twins.

Molitor retired after the 1998 season, staying on with the Twins as a coach from 1999 to 2001. In January 2004 he was voted into the Baseball Hall of Fame on the first ballot. Ever active in the world of baseball, Molitor recently became the batting coach for the Seattle Mariners.

PAUL MOLITOR

HIGH SCHOOL

(1973–1974) Paul Molitor is the cadet colonel at Cretin High School, a Catholic all-boys school. He was a standout in basketball and baseball for the schools' team, the Raiders.

UNIVERSITY OF MINNESOTA

(1974–1978) Molitor turns down offers to play professional baseball. He decides to go to college and play baseball for coach Dick Siebert at the University of Minnesota.

WORLD SERIES: BREWERS

(1982) Molitor's incredible display of hitting is not enough for the Milwaukee Brewers. The St. Louis Cardinals win the World Series in seven games.

WORLD SERIES: BLUE JAYS

(1993) Eleven years after his first World Series, Molitor sets World Series records with twelve hits, ten runs, six stolen bases, two triples, six extra base hits, and a .500 batting average. He is named the series Most Valuable Player.

MINNESOTA TWINS

(1996) As a member of the Minnesota Twins, Molitor hits a triple into the right field corner for his 3,000th career hit.

KIRBY PUCKETT

STUNNING START

(1984) Kirby Puckett has four hits in his first major league game. He is only the sixth player in American League history to do it.

TWINS/BRAVES

(1991) With game six of the World Series tied, Puckett is the hero as his eleventh-inning home run sails over the wall at the Metrodome.

TEN-YEAR TOTAL

(1984–1994) His 2,040 hits rank him second all time behind Willie Keeler for the most hits during a player's first ten major league seasons.

49

Herb Brooks

DURING HIS STUDENT YEARS, Herb Brooks was the fastest skater on the University of Minnesota hockey team, but he wasn't quite good enough to make the 1960 U.S. Olympic squad. He was the last player cut during try-outs, in fact, and when the U.S. team went on to win the gold medal, Brooks's father told him it looked like they eliminated the right guy.

Born and raised on St. Paul's East Side, Brooks attended Johnson High School, where he led the school to the 1955 Minnesota State Hockey Championship. After being cut from the 1960 Olympic team, Brooks focused on academics, earning his bachelor's degree in psychology in 1961. He continued to play hockey, however, and the swift-skating forward made both the 1964 and 1968 U.S. Olympic teams.

Eventually Brooks returned to coach hockey at the University of Minnesota, and within seven years his teams had won three national championships. He left the university in 1979 and returned to Olympic competition, this time as coach. Thirteen native Minnesotans were selected to the 1980 team, and Brooks appointed former Boston University star Mike Eruzione the team captain. They were young and small, but on the strength of good skating and Jim Craig's reliable goaltending, the shaggy, youthful team tied with Sweden and went on to victories over Czechoslovakia, West Germany, and Norway. In the medal round, with the entire nation behind them, Team USA defeated a strong Russian team 4–3, and a few days later they topped Finland on a pair of goals by Mark Johnson to complete their "miracle on ice." They had won the gold medal.

Following his Olympic triumph, Brooks coached in Davos, Switzerland, and then with the New York Rangers. Brooks encouraged the Rangers to use a creative, weaving European style of play, and became the National Hockey League coach of the year in 1981–1982. During his three years with the club he led the Rangers to 100 wins in the shortest amount of time in club history.

In later life Brooks coached and scouted hockey for several teams, including the Minnesota North Stars, St. Cloud State University, the New Jersey Devils, Team France, and the Pittsburgh Penguins. Brooks was again chosen to coach Team USA at the 2002 Winter Olympics in Salt Lake City, Utah. His team played well but fell to Canada 5–2 in the gold medal round. After the silver medal win Brooks returned to work as a scout for Mario LeMieux and the Pittsburgh Penguins. His name continued to surface as a candidate for head coaching jobs in the NHL until he was tragically killed on the freeway in the fall of 2003, returning home from a round of golf.

Neal Broten

NEIL BROTEN HAS HAD A STORYBOOK career. Only five foot seven inches tall and 145 pounds, the ninth-grader from Roseau won the hearts of Minnesotans during his first state tournament appearance, proving that he could survive among bigger, stronger players. Broten went on to lead the University of Minnesota Gophers to the national championship in 1979.

A year later, Broten and Team USA skated to the Gold Medal at the Lake Placid Olympics. In 1981 Broten received the first Hobey Baker Award, presented by the Decathlon Athletic Club to the best college hockey player in the country. That same year the Gophers lost to the University of Wisconsin in the national championship game.

Broten didn't have time to pout; he joined the North Stars just in time for a Stanley Cup play-off run. The Stars advanced to the Stanley Cup finals for the first time in franchise history, defeating the Boston Bruins, the Buffalo Sabres, and the Calgary Flames, before falling to the defending champion New York Islanders, four games to one.

Broten didn't return to the cup finals until 1991, when the Stars succumbed to the Pittsburgh Penguins four games to two.

When the Stars moved to Texas in 1993, Broten contemplated retirement, but eventually agreed to move with his family to Dallas. In 1995 he made it to the Stanley Cup finals for a third time, helping the New Jersey Devils sweep the Detroit Red Wings. With this he became the first player in the history of the sport to win an NCAA championship, an Olympic Gold Medal, and a Stanley Cup.

Broten retired from hockey in 1997. He and his wife Sally, who is also from Roseau, have three daughters; they own a horse farm in River Falls, Wisconsin.

Phil Housley

PHIL HOUSLEY WAS PART of Doug Woog's South St. Paul High School state hockey tournament teams of the early 1980s. Housley was a heads-up defenseman and was drafted by the Buffalo Sabres with the sixth overall pick of the 1982 NHL draft.

Housley made the difficult jump directly from high school to the NHL successfully. In fact, he went on to play in seven all-star games and became the highest scoring American player in the history of the NHL. He trails only Paul Coffey and Ray Borque in career assists.

Always one of the best skaters on the ice, Housley won a World Cup championship with the Team USA in 1996 and a silver medal in the 2002 Winter Olympics. He has played with seven different teams during his long career, including eighty games with the Chicago Blackhawks in 2001–2002. Housley was traded to the Toronto Maple Leafs during the 2003 season, and he retired recently to spend more time with his family.

PHIL HOUSLEY

ST. PAUL CIVIC CENTER

(1980–1981) The South St. Paul High School Packer's Phil Housley is the best hockey player in the widely watched Minnesota tournament.

ST. PAUL VULCANS

(1982) As a tune-up for the rougher, tougher NHL, Housley plays with the U.S. Hockey League Vulcans.

DRAFTED SIXTH OVERALL

(1982) The NHL's Buffalo Sabres draft Housley in the first round.

HIGHEST SCORING AMERICAN

(1999) Housley is credited with three assists on March 17 while playing with the Calgary Flames. This brings his career point total to 1,066 and makes him the highest scoring U.S.-born player in the history of the NHL.

SALT LAKE CITY

(2002) Housley plays well in the Olympics and Team USA wins a silver medal, its first in more than twenty years.

53

Briana Scurry

AT THE 1996 SUMMER OLYMPICS in Atlanta, Georgia, soccer goalkeeper Briana Scurry's save of Team China's third penalty kick turned the tide, and Team USA went on to win its first the gold medal.

Scurry's soccer career began at Anoka High School, where she led the Tornados to the 1989 Minnesota girls state soccer championship. Named the top female athlete in Minnesota, she also received All-American honors. Scurry attended the University of Massachusetts and became the premier college goalkeeper in the nation, winning two national goalkeeper of the year awards. She graduated in 1995 with a bachelor's degree in political science.

In big games Scurry has been outstanding. She had four wins, zero losses, and one tie at the 1996 Olympics and five wins, zero losses, and one tie in the 1999 World Cup.

In 2004 Scurry was stellar as starting goalie for Team USA. The U.S. women's soccer team regained their Gold Medal status. She also continued to play for the Atlanta Beat of the Women's United Soccer Association until that league's unfortunate demise.

BORN IN ST. PAUL IN 1971, Tony Sanneh learned about soccer from his father, who is from Gambia, West Africa. Sanneh attended St. Paul Academy (SPA), a longtime Minnesota high school soccer power, and helped the Spartans win state championships in his freshman and sophomore seasons. The Spartans lost in the semifinals his junior year, and in his senior year they were beaten in the state championship game by Apple Valley High School.

He continued to be one of the best young players in the nation. In 1990 while playing for the St. Paul Blackhawks he won the McGuire Cup, a national junior challenge cup for boys under the age of nineteen. He then attended the University of Wisconsin-Milwaukee, where he played for four seasons and became their all-time leading scorer. His professional career began in 1994 with the Milwaukee Rampage of the United Soccer Leagues. He played indoor soccer for the Chicago Power in 1994–1995 and went on to play for the Minnesota Thunder in 1995–1996, an A-level team.

After this Sanneh became a mainstay with DC United, and as a right midfielder he scored twenty goals and thirty-two assists over three seasons with the major league soccer team, winning championships in 1996 and 1997. He later signed a multimillion dollar deal with Hertha Berlin of the German national league. Sanneh played in front of huge crowds in Berlin, at the Olympic Stadium.

Sanneh played for Hertha Berlin for three seasons before transferring to FC Nurenberg and became a starter for them as well. He was a member of the U.S. national team in the 2002 World Cup, playing in Korea and Japan. The right back spot was claimed by Sanneh, who would play every minute of every game and was named one of the top eleven players of the World Cup. Sanneh returned to play for FC Nurnberg for the 2002–2003 season and was a starter when healthy. A back injury kept him out of several games, but he returned to the lineup in 2004 and the team regained their first division status. After a lengthy discussion with family members, Sanneh turned down the contract he was offered and chose instead to play with the Columbus Crew of the MLS so that he could be closer to friends and family.

Tony Sanneh

GRIDIRON

(1974–1978) Tom Lehman is the signal caller on the Alexandria High School football team. He considers going to St. John's College and playing football for legendary coach John Gagliardi, but chooses the University of Minnesota instead.

UNIVERSITY GOLF TEAM

(1978–1982) Lehman is named All-Big-Ten and All-American golfer. He graduates with a bachelor's degree in accounting.

MINNESOTA STATE AMATEUR CHAMPION

(1981) Twenty-two-year-old Lehman wins the tournament and is ranked among the top ten nationwide.

DECISION TIME

(1990) Lehman, who for several years played on the Ben Hogan Tour, considers coaching the University of Minnesota Golf team, but later withdraws his name.

NUMBER ONE

(1997) The low-key "linkster" becomes the world's number-one golfer in 1997.

PATTY BERG

AMATEUR GOLFING CHAMP

(1934) Patty Berg wins the Minneapolis City Championship. It is the first of her twenty-eight amateur wins.

CURTIS CUP

(1936, 1938) Berg is a member of the U.S. Curtis Cup team.

LADIES PROFESSIONAL GOLF ASSOCIATION

(1948) Berg is one of the founders and a charter member of the LPGA.

U.S. OPEN

(1959) Her hole in one at the U.S. Open at Churchill Valley Country Club in Pittsburgh is the first ever by a woman at a PGA event.

BORN IN AUSTIN, MINNESOTA, Tom Lehman later moved with his family to Alexandria. Tom attended the University of Minnesota, graduating in 1982. A star of the golf team, he was named All-Big-Ten and All-American golfer while attending the university, and he decided to make a career of the sport. Lehman had little success on the Professional Golf Association (PGA) Tour, however, and wound up playing on the Ben Hogan Tour (since renamed the Buy.com Tour) for nearly ten years.

In 1990 Lehman was offered the golf-coaching job at the University of Minnesota, but he turned it down to continue his dream of playing on the PGA Tour. The next year on the Ben Hogan Tour he was named Player of the Year, and this distinction granted him much freer entry to PGA tournaments. He showed continued and significant improvement in these events and steadily moved up the leader board at big tournaments. In April 1993 he finished third at the Masters Golf Tournament at Augusta National Golf Club in Georgia. The next year he finished an impressive second at the same tournament.

Lehman's first PGA Tour win came in 1994 at the Memorial Golf Tournament. Later that year Lehman won the Colonial Open with a twenty under par. As a result of his outstanding play he was selected to represent the United States in the Ryder Cup.

In 1996, after falling short in the final round of several of the majors, Lehman won the British Open at Royal Lytham and St. Anne's. He also captured the Tour Championship that year, and was named PGA Player of the Year. One year later he became the number-one golfer in the world.

Since then Lehman has slowly declined in the rankings, yet he remains a tour favorite, as much for his warm personality as for his remarkable strokes. Lehman and his family live in Scottsdale, Arizona.

Lehman was recently chosen as Captain of the American Ryder Cup team which will compete in Ireland in 2006.

Patty Berg

PATTY BERG WAS AS COMPETITIVE as they come. As a teenager she was the quarterback with the Fiftieth Street Tigers, an otherwise all-boy neighborhood team in South Minneapolis. She competed in a variety of sports as a girl and won a national medal in speed skating.

The freckle-faced redhead got her start at golf at Interlachen Country Club in Edina. She played her first tournament at age thirteen and was soon winning them. After her twenty-eighth amateur tournament victory, Berg became a professional in 1940 at age twenty-one.

Following a wartime stint in the U.S. Marines, Berg returned to the sport, and in 1948 she became a founder and first president of the Ladies Professional Golf Association. She went on to win fifty-seven tournaments, fifteen of which were majors. She was named the Associated Press Woman Athlete of the Year in 1938, 1943, and 1955.

Berg's illustrious career was topped off when she was inducted into the World Golf Hall of Fame at Pinehurst, North Carolina, in 1974. The other golfers inducted with her that day were Jack Nicklaus, Ben Hogan, Arnold Palmer, Sam Snead, Byron Nelson, Gary Player, and Gene Sarazen. In 1995 the Professional Golf Association (PGA) honored Berg with its Distinguished Service Award. Patty owns a home in Lakeville, Minnesota.

Patty Berg's illustrious career was topped off when she was inducted into the World Golf Hall of Fame at Pinehurst, North Carolina, in 1974.

BIRTH

Born August 7, 1945,
in Canton, Ohio.

**UNIVERSITY OF
NOTRE DAME**

(1966) Alan Page anchors
a tough defense and the
Notre Dame Irish win the
national championship.

DRAFTED BY THE VIKINGS

(1967) Vikings general
manager Mike Finks
makes Page the Vikings'
number-one draft pick.

**DOMINATING
DEFENSIVE TACKLE**

(1971) Page is clearly
superior to all other players
in the National Football
League and becomes the
first defensive player to be
named the Most Valuable
Player.

LAW DEGREE

(1978) After bringing on the
ire of Vikings head coach
Bud Grant by reporting late
for training camp, Page
receives his JD degree from
the University of Minnesota.

**THE HONORABLE
ALAN PAGE**

(1993) Page is sworn in
and becomes a Minnesota
associate justice.

Alan
Page

ALAN PAGE, A NOTRE DAME alumnus, was the first defensive player in the history of the National Football League (NFL) to win the Most Valuable Player award. A first-round draft pick for the Minnesota Vikings in 1967, the big defensive tackle often dominated games with his quickness, playing sideline to sideline. Page had great anticipation off the ball, and he would occasionally tackle the ball carrier during the hand-off. Ends Jim Marshall and Carl Eller often helped Page arrive at the quarterback for the successful sack. This formidable trio, along with Gary Larson and Doug Sutherland, made up the Vikings' legendary Purple People Eaters. A solid line-backing trio and a secondary led by free safety Paul Krause made the Viking's defense one of the best in football during Page's era. Page himself came up with the ball twenty-three times after their bruising rush had caused fumbles.

A quiet leader, he was National Football Conference Defensive Player of the Year four times and the NFL Most Valuable Player in 1971. The Vikings played in four Super Bowls during his tenure, and although they were soundly defeated by their opponents in all four games, they will forever be enshrined for their continued success during those years.

Page went on to earn his juris doctor from the University of Minnesota Law School in 1978 while continuing his football career. His last four seasons were with the Chicago Bears. After retiring in 1981, he joined the law firm of Lindquist and Venum. In 1987 Page became an assistant attorney general of the State of Minnesota, and five years later he became an associate justice of the Minnesota Supreme Court. These days he can often be seen jogging around Minneapolis lakes.

Page became an assistant attorney general of the State of Minnesota, and four years later he became an associate justice of the Minnesota Supreme Court.

Tom Malchow

WHEN TOM MALCHOW JUMPED into the water his cousins would yell, "Big Dog's in the pool." That big dog grew up to be a six-foot-six Olympic swimmer.

Malchow was born in St. Paul and attended St. Thomas Academy. He led the school to a state swimming championship and in the process set numerous school and state swimming records. He is a graduate of the University of Michigan.

He won the silver medal at the 1996 Summer Olympics in Atlanta, Georgia, and four years later won the gold medal at the 2000 Summer Olympics in Sydney, Australia. Later that year Big Dog broke the world record in the 200-meter butterfly.

Malchow was eager to defend his medal at the 2004 Olympics in Athens, Greece, but he was diagnosed with a torn shoulder tendon after qualifying at the U.S. trials. He reached the finals in the butterfly once again, but failed to medal, though he did help the U.S. freestyle relay team to a bronze medal.

When Tom Malchow jumped into the water his cousins would yell, "Big Dog's in the pool." That big dog grew up to be a 6-foot-six Olympic swimmer.

Greg Lemond

IN 1986 GREG LEMOND became the first American ever to win the grueling Tour de France bicycling race. He won it again in 1989 and 1990.

Lemond's first victory stunned the cycling world simply because no American had ever proven tough enough to pull off such a feat, but the second was no less shocking. During the off-season Lemond had been accidentally shot by his brother-in-law while turkey hunting. The buckshot entered the lining of Lemond's heart and he almost bled to death. Fortunately, he recovered, but the likelihood of racing again professionally looked dim.

Yet a year later he was back in France competing again with the world's cycling elite. The race went down to the final day—an individual time-trial—with two-time winner Laurent Fignon holding a seemingly insurmountable lead of fifty seconds. Pedaling in the rain, Lemond cut fifty-one seconds off Fignon's time, and emerged with a second unexpected victory. The win landed Lemond on the cover of *Sports Illustrated*, bringing national attention to his sport. Six months later he was awarded the beautiful Grecian Amphora vase for being named Sportsman of the Year by the magazine.

In 1990 Lemond won his third and final Tour de France. A few years later he retired from the sport because of a cellular disorder (mitochondrio myopathy), which made him too lethargic to race.

Since retiring Lemond has participated in FF2000 car racing and charity bike races. He and his wife, Kathy, and their three children live in Medina, Minnesota.

WHEN HARMON KILLEBREW RETIRED from baseball in 1975, he had hit 573 home runs—more than any other American League right-handed hitter in history. But his career didn't begin on such a high note. When the Washington Senators moved to Minnesota in 1960 and became the Twins, Killebrew was known for hitting pop-ups that looked like home runs until they fell into the glove of an opposing player. As he settled into his new hometown, fans anxiously waited for him to improve. He did, and he soon became a fan favorite.

When Killebrew climbed out of the dugout and took his place in the on-deck circle, everyone in the stadium noticed. He wore number three, the same jersey number as Babe Ruth. Fans knew they might see a home run, and often they did: the excitement was real.

Killebrew's home runs usually lifted above the lights before descending into the left field bleachers. He hit one once in every 14.22 bats, on average, trailing only Babe Ruth, Mark McGuire, and Ralph Kiner. His best season was 1969, when he hit 49 homers and knocked in 145 runs for the Billy Martin-managed Twins. The Twins won the American League West that year and Killebrew was named the American League Most Valuable Player.

After his retirement in 1975 Killebrew went into broadcasting. He was a color commentator during Twins' games for several years. Since leaving the booth he has stayed in touch with the team. At Twins Fest, held annually at the Metrodome, the gentle plainspoken athlete known as "Killer," one of the best power hitters of all time, can still be seen signing autographs.

Harmon Killebrew

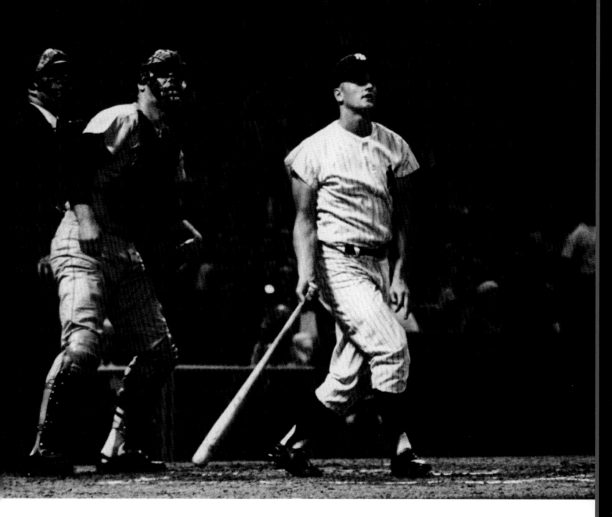

Roger Maris

ROGER MARIS WAS BORN in Hibbing, Minnesota, to first-generation Croatian parents. He grew up in Fargo, North Dakota, where he was a great high school baseball player. Named the Legion Player of the Year in 1953, Maris later signed with the Cleveland Indians, who assigned him to their Fargo farm club.

Maris received his call-up to the majors in 1957. The Indians traded him to Kansas City, who in turn traded him to the New York Yankees. In 1961 he broke the single-season home-run record when he swatted sixty-one round-trippers. Maris finished his career with the St. Louis Cardinals, playing

two seasons with the National League team before retiring in 1968.

The media attention Maris received in 1961 was something he was not quite accustomed to, and since then there have been numerous accounts of his conquest of Babe Ruth's single-season home-run record.

Although he is not in the National Baseball Hall of Fame, the quiet slugger will be remembered in baseball history for that remarkable accomplishment. Maris died from cancer at the age of fifty-one in Gainesville, Florida. He was buried in Fargo.

Bronko Nagurski

BRONKO NAGURSKI HAD A RING size of 22 and a reputation for bone-jarring tackles that frequently caused fumbles. During an era when defensive linemen often weighed in at 210, Nagurski tipped the scales at 230 or more, which may explain why, as a running back, he often left the bodies of would-be tacklers strewn in his path.

Born in Rainy River, Ontario, Nagurski grew up across the border in International Falls, Minnesota. He attended the University of Minnesota where he was an All-American fullback and tackle for the Gophers. A star running back for the Chicago Bears, Nagurski played in three NFL championships in Chicago. He successfully completed two passes for touchdowns in the 1933 championship game.

The big, rugged ball carrier retired in 1937 to devote more time to professional wrestling. He didn't enjoy the sport but times were hard and he had a family to support.

In 1943 Nagurski came out of retirement to play one more season with the Bears, contributing to yet another NFL title. He was inducted into the Pro Football Hall of Fame as a charter member in 1963, and he was also named to the NFL seventy-fifth anniversary team. *Sports Illustrated* recently included him on a list of the ten best big running backs of all time, for his ferocity, size, and quickness.

After his retirement Nagurski lived quietly in International Falls, where he owned a gas station until his death in 1990.

In 1943 Nagurski came out of retirement to play one more season with the Bears, contributing to yet another NFL title. He was inducted into the Pro Football Hall of Fame as a charter member in 1963, and he was also named to the NFL seventy-fifth anniversary team.

Vern Gagne

VERNE GAGNE, A PIONEER in the sport of professional wrestling, attended Robbinsdale High School and the University of Minnesota, where he starred on the football team during the twilight of Bernie Bierman's long coaching career. He also excelled at wrestling, winning the NCAA national title two years running in his weight class. Gagne was chosen as an alternate for the 1948 Olympic games, and after a brief stint with the Green Bay Packers, he turned to professional wrestling as a career. His match with then-world-champion Lou Thesz, on October 27, 1951, is often referred to as the greatest wrestling match of all time. The two fought to a draw, however, and Thesz retained his title.

Two years later Gagne won the first of many professional titles. He held the U.S. belt from 1958 to 1960. Following a controversy with the National Wrestling Association, however, Gagne formed a rival organization, the American Wrestling Association (AWA), and he won the first of ten AWA World Heavyweight Championships later that year. During the following decade—a golden age of professional wrestling—Gagne engaged in classic bouts with The Crusher, Fritz Von Erich, Mad Dog Vachon, Dick the Bruiser, Dr. X, and other now-legendary athletes. A wrestler's wrestler, Gagne knew all the holds, and invariably played the role of Mr. Clean against his more colorful, but also more underhanded, opponents.

The tireless Gagne won his final AWA Title in 1980, in front of 20,000 screaming fans at Commisky Park, Chicago, and retired a year later, after yet another successful title defense.

At the peak of Gagne's dominance in pro wrestling, he won seven consecutive championships. He was a pro wrestler for nearly thirty years, winning his last title in 1980.

BRONKO NAGURSKI

UNIVERSITY OF MINNESOTA
(1927-1929) Nagurski is named All-American fullback and tackle.

FIRST OFFICIAL NFL CHAMPIONSHIP GAME
(1933) Playing at fullback for the Chicago Bears, Nagurski leads the team to its first NFL title.

WRESTLING
(1937) Bronko retires from football and wins the World Heavyweight Wrestling title later the same year.

PRO FOOTBALL HALL OF FAME
(1963) The venerable Nagurski becomes a charter member of the Pro Football Hall of Fame.

THE NAGURSKI AWARD
(2003) The Nagurski Award is given to the best defensive player in football.

VERN GAGNE

HIGH SCHOOL
(1943) Gagne graduates from Robinsdale High School and is widely considered to be one of the best prep athletes in Minnesota.

UNIVERSITY OF MINNESOTA
(1944) As a freshman Gagne wins the Big-Ten heavyweight wrestling championship.

BIERMAN'S LEATHERNECKS
(1949) After serving in the Marine Corps during World War II, Gagne returns to the University of Minnesota, plays an end on the football team, and is named to the college all-star team.

PRO WRESTLING
(1950) A fledgling, weekly television show called All-Star Wrestling debuts as Gagne begins his pro career.

STEPS AWAY FROM THE RING
(1981) The legacy is handed down to Gagne's son, Greg, and Vern retires having won a record ten All-Star Wrestling Association championships.

Dave Winfield

ST. PAUL NATIVE DAVE WINFIELD began his life in sports on the Oxford Playground baseball team, a block from his house in what was then the St. Paul ghetto. Winfield went on to attend St. Paul Central High School and the University of Minnesota, where he played both baseball and basketball. He was a power forward on coach Bill Musselman's 1971–72 championship Big Ten basketball team and a star pitcher for Dick Siebert's baseball team, which also won the league championship.

Winfield was drafted by teams in three professional sports—the Atlanta Hawks of the NBA, the Minnesota Vikings of the NFL, and the San Diego Padres of baseball's National League. Winfield chose baseball. Despite his excellent pitching skills, the Padres decided they wanted his bat in the lineup, so they moved him to the outfield, where Winfield became a sensational fielder with good range and a great arm. In fact, he won seven Gold Glove awards at his new position, and was a perennial all star, as both a Padre (1979–1980), and a New York Yankee (1981–1988).

Winfield's disputes with owner George Steinbrenner made his years in New York stormy ones, but on the field he continued to perform well. Hitting with both consistency and power, he became the first Yankee since Yogi Berra to hit more than 100 RBIs for five consecutive seasons.

Following back surgery, a year-long hiatus from the sport, and a trade to the California Angels, Winfield was chosen as Comeback Player of the Year in 1990. Perhaps the highlight of his career was the 1992 World Series, however, when he had the winning hit for the Toronto Blue Jays in the eleventh inning that won both the game and the series.

Winfield ended his career with the Minnesota Twins, where he collected his milestone 3,000th career hit. He ranks among the all-time leaders in hits, doubles, and home runs. After his retirement in 1995 Winfield had a short but successful career in broadcasting with Fox television. He has authored a book, *Winfield: A Player's Life*, and was devoted throughout his playing career to charitable activities. In 2001 he was elected to the National Baseball Hall of Fame.

Winfield was drafted by teams in three professional sports—the Atlanta Hawks of the NBA, the Minnesota Vikings of the NFL, and the San Diego Padres of baseball's National League. Winfield chose baseball.

MADDEN COACHED THE Oakland Raiders to a win in the 1977 Super Bowl over the Minnesota Vikings. Madden was born in Austin, Minnesota, on April 10, 1936. The family moved to California when Madden was six years old. Madden attended San Mateo High School with John Robinson, and both of them received athletic scholarships to the University of Oregon. Madden eventually left to play tackle at California Polytechnic Institute and at San Mateo University. Both Madden and Robinson would later become great NFL coaches.

The Philadelphia Eagles drafted Madden in 1960, but he injured a knee in training camp. While rehabilitating the knee, Madden spent a good deal of time watching films and learning more about the game. He was eventually cut from the squad, and he went back to California, where he obtained a master's degree in education from San Mateo University.

Madden became the linebacker coach of the Oakland Raiders in 1967, and he was named head coach in 1969 by Al Davis, the Raider's owner. He immediately set the Raiders on a winning course, winning seven Western Division titles during his ten seasons. But in those days, though the Raiders were good, the Miami Dolphins and the Pittsburgh Steelers were often better. In fact, the Dolphins and the Steelers represented the American Football Conference in seven Super Bowls during the 1970s. The Raiders played in the Super Bowl in 1977, defeating the Minnesota Vikings 37–14.

In 1978 Madden retired from coaching, having built up an extraordinary 112-39-7 record and a .731 winning percentage. Since then he has become a popular football television commentator with CBS and FOX. Madden joined the ABC *Monday Night Football* broadcast in 2002, teaming with play-by-play man Al Michaels.

John Madden

BUD GRANT OUTLAWED GLOVES and choppers at the chilly outdoor Metropolitan Stadium in Bloomington, but the cold weather was a huge advantage for his team. The Minnesota Vikings were virtually unbeatable at that stadium and made it to four Super Bowls under his lead. Grant was head coach of the Vikings for eighteen seasons (1967 to 1983 and again in 1985), and during that time his teams won eleven division championships and four NFL National Football Conference titles.

Grant was born on May 20, 1927, in Superior, Wisconsin. He attended Superior High School, where he excelled at football, baseball, and basketball.

During World War II Grant attended the Great Lakes Naval Academy, where he was coached by football legend Paul Brown. After the war Grant attended the University of Minnesota and played end for coach Bernie Bierman. An All-Big-Ten selection in both football and basketball, Grant went on to excel at both sports on the professional level. He earned all-pro honors in the NFL with the Philadelphia Eagles, and he also played basketball for the Minneapolis Lakers.

Grant eventually left the Eagles to play football for the Winnipeg Blue Bombers of the Canadian Football League, where he remained for ten years, first as a player and later as a coach. In 1967 he became the head coach of the Minnesota Vikings, where his stoic sideline persona became legendary. Television cameras lingered on his expressionless face as his team made their way to victory at Metropolitan Stadium.

Grant retired from coaching in 1985. Five of his former top players are in the Pro Football Hall of Fame: quarterback Fran Tarkenton, offensive tackle Ron Yary, defensive free safety Paul Krause, defensive tackle Alan Page, and defensive end Carl Eller. Grant was inducted into the Hall of Fame in 1994.

Grant lives in Bloomington with his wife. He remains an avid outdoorsman, hunting from the duck blinds any chance he gets. Grant's son Mike has coached the Eden Prairie High School football team to several Minnesota state championships.

Grant was head coach of the Vikings for eighteen seasons (1967 to 1983 and again in 1985), and during that time his teams won eleven division championships and four NFL National Football Conference titles.

Bud Grant

Charles Bender

CHARLES BENDER PITCHED in five World Series for the Philadelphia Athletics and was the winning pitcher in six World Series games. He is credited with inventing the nickel curve, also known as the slider.

Bender, an Ojibwe, was born on the White Earth Indian Reservation in central Minnesota on May 5, 1883. As a child he was sent to Pennsylvania to attend the Carlisle School for Indians. He began playing major league baseball for the Athletics in 1905, when legendary manager Connie Mack was in charge, and Bender soon received the nickname "Chief" because of his Indian heritage. He pitched a no-hitter in 1910. In addition to pitching, Bender also played first base and outfield, and he was used as a pinch hitter.

Bender later played for the Baltimore Terrapins in the Federal League and returned to the major leagues with the Philadelphia Phillies in 1916. He retired in 1917, but continued to manage and scout. He was coach of the U.S. Naval Academy for five years, pitched in the Middle Atlantic League, and scouted for the New York Yankees, the Philadelphia Athletics, and the New York Giants. He eventually married and became a renaissance man of sorts, reading classic literature, painting in oils, and becoming an expert in textiles. He was elected into the Baseball Hall of Fame in 1953, and he died a year later.

Rod Carew

ONE OF THE BEST BASEBALL HITTERS ever to play the game, Rod Carew reached bases safely in every way imaginable. He hit line drives, slapped ground balls that died just past the infield, lofted triples, and sliced laser-like doubles. He was the consummate American League batter during the 1970s.

Carew was an amazing bunter. He would drag, bunt the ball in between the pitcher and the first baseman, and while the ball rolled to a stop at the back of the bright infield grass the swift-running Carew would be reaching first base safely.

Carew played for the Minnesota Twins from 1967 to 1978. During that time he won seven American League batting titles. (Only Ty Cobb, Tony Guinn, and Honus Wagner have more batting crowns than Carew.) In the field, he began as a second baseman but later settled in at first base, where he spent the remainder of his career.

Carew's most impressive season came in 1977, the year he appeared on the cover of *Sports Illustrated* with Ted Williams. His batting average remained above .400 for most of that summer, and he finished the year at .388, the highest percentage since Williams hit .406 in 1941. Carew was voted the American League Most Valuable Player that year, with 128 runs scored, 239 hits, and 16 triples.

Carew finished up his career with the California Angels, where he continued to hit well over .300; he was named to eighteen straight all-star games in the course of his stellar career.

After retiring, Carew served as the Angels' batting instructor for eight seasons. The Milwaukee Brewers hired Carew as their batting coach in 2000, and Brewer hitters responded by setting the team record for home runs.

Carew was inducted into the National Baseball Hall of Fame in 1991. The Minnesota Twins retired his jersey, number 29, and a huge picture of Carew hangs inside the Metrodome.

CHARLES BENDER

WORLD SERIES

(1905) Bender pitches a shutout at the first official World Series, played in 1905 between the New York Giants and the Philadelphia Athletics. It is the only win for the Athletics during the series.

LEAGUE LEADER

(1910, 1914) The hurler pitches better than anyone else in the American League. He tallies twenty-three wins and five losses in 1910 and an impressive seventeen and three record in 1914.

HIS LAST WORLD SERIES

(1913) In a game against the New York Giants at the Polo Grounds, Bender survives a hitting onslaught and hangs on for a 6–4 victory. He also wins game four. The Athletics wrap up the series with a win in game five.

ROD CAREW

SANDLOT BALL

(1964) Twins' scout Herb Stein discovers Rod Carew as he plays baseball in New York City.

OPENING DAY

(1967) At the tender age of twenty-one, Carew is the opening-day second basemen for the Minnesota Twins.

BATTING CHAMP

(1977) Carew wins his sixth American League batting title with an incredible .388 batting average.

TRADED TO THE ANGELS

(1979) Carew is traded to the California Angels.

NUMBER 29

(1990s) Both the Angels and the Twins retire Carew's jersey number 29.

GEORGE MIKAN

DEPAUL

(1945) George Mikan is the talk of college basketball in 1945. The Blue Demons win the National Invitational Tournament (NIT) at Madison Square Garden. The NIT is considered to be a better tournament than the National Collegiate Athletic Association (NCAA).

NBA CHAMPIONS

(1952–1954) Led by center Mikan, power forward Vern Mikkelson, and guard Slater Martin, the Lakers win three consecutive NBA titles.

COMMISSIONER MIKAN

(1967) Mikan is named commissioner of the American Basketball Association.

NBA FIFTIETH ANNIVERSARY TEAM

(1996) Mikan is named to the commemorative list for the NBA's fiftieth anniversary team. Also included among the fifty chosen is his former Laker teammate Slater Martin, and their former coach, John Kundla.

TOP TEN DYNASTY

(2002) ESPN names the Minneapolis Lakers one of the top ten dynasties in the history of sports.

George Mikan

THE MARQUEE OUTSIDE Madison Square Garden in New York City once read "Knicks vs. Mikan" instead of Knicks vs. Lakers. That's how good a basketball player George Mikan was. Mikan joined the NBA in the early 1950s with the Minneapolis Lakers. They called him "Mr. Basketball."

At 6-foot, 10-inches and 245 pounds, Mikan was intimidating and fiercely competitive. He led the league in personal fouls for three years, but also transformed the sport. As Sid Hartman, longtime columnist for the *Minneapolis Star-Tribune*, noted, his dominance forced more rule changes than any other athlete in basketball history: Goal-tending was outlawed, the lane was widened from 6 to 12 feet, and the 24-second clock was established.

But nothing could stop Mikan in his prime. The Minneapolis Lakers won four NBA championships while he was in the lineup. He retired after leading his team to the 1954 title.

Already an attorney, Mikan practiced law for the next thirteen years. He was commissioner of the American Basketball Association from 1967 to 1969. It was Mikan's decision to use red-white-and-blue basketballs.

In the mid-1980s Mikan led the task force that eventually brought an NBA expansion team, the Timberwolves, to Minnesota. In turn, the state has memorialized him with a life-size statue in Target Center in downtown Minneapolis. Mikan has been inducted into the Basketball Hall of Fame, as have two of his former teammates, Slater Martin and Vern Mikkelson, and coach John Kundla. When, in 1996, the NBA announced its fiftieth anniversary team, Mikan and Martin were two of the top fifty players.

Mikan, a longtime resident of Edina, Minnesota, moved to Scottsdale, Arizona, in 2000. Mikan died in 2005.

Kevin McHale

KEVIN MCHALE WAS ONE of the best players in the history of basketball. The dominating forward was selected to the NBA fiftieth anniversary team and to the Basketball Hall of Fame.

During his high school years in Hibbing, McHale led the Blue Jackets to state tournament appearances in 1975 and 1976. McHale went on to an All-American career with the University of Minnesota Golden Gophers.

The six-foot-ten forward was the Boston Celtics' third pick in the first round of the 1980 NBA draft. Though a reserve in his first season, he helped the team win the NBA championship, and during the off-season McHale married his high school girlfriend Lynn, a graduate of the University of St. Thomas.

In the course of the 1980s the trio of McHale, Larry Byrd, and Robert Parish became legendary, as the Celtics won six conference titles and three NBA championships. At the peak of his career McHale himself was virtually unstoppable. He once scored fifty-six points in a single game against the Detroit Pistons. The dazzling array of low-post moves he developed revolutionized pivot play.

McHale retired after a thirteen-year career and moved back to Minnesota. He later became the vice president of basketball operations for the Minnesota Timberwolves, where for many years he worked closely with coach Flip Saunders, with whom he had played on the 1976–1977 University of Minnesota basketball team. McHale, his wife Lynn, and their children live in North Oaks, Minnesota.

KEVIN MCHALE

STATE BASKETBALL TOURNAMENT

(1976) In the class AA state championship game, Kevin McHale is not enough for Hibbing to overcome the undefeated Bloomington Jefferson Jaguars. Hibbing is defeated 60–51.

GOLDEN GOPHERS

(1976–1977) The team is on probation. McHale (class of 1980), center Mychael Thompson (class of 1977), and guard Ray Williams (class of 1977) later become NBA lottery picks.

THE BOSTON CELTICS

(1980) With their envious first round position (third overall) the Celtics draft McHale.

NBA CHAMPIONS

(1981) McHale comes off the bench to spark the Celtics, who trail the Philadelphia 76'ers three to one in the Eastern Conference finals. The Celtics fight back, win the series, and go on to defeat the Houston Rockets for the title.

NBA 50TH ANNIVERSARY TEAM

(1996) A prolific scorer throughout his career, McHale is one of top fifty players of all time.

THE MAYO BROTHERS

ROCHESTER

(1863) Dr. William Mayo moves to Rochester, Minnesota, and is appointed the examining surgeon for the Union Army.

WILLIAM JR.

(1883) Mayo's son William graduates from medical school at the University of Michigan and joins his father's medical practice.

DISASTER

(1883) A tornado turns Rochester upside down. With help from the Sisters of St. Francis nuns, the elder Dr. Mayo works on the injured.

CHARLES

(1888) Charles, the second son, graduates from medical school at Northwestern University. He too joins his father's practice.

SISTERS OF ST. FRANCIS

(1889) The nuns raise money for the construction of a hospital. Dr. William Mayo is asked to serve as the chief physician.

MAYO FOUNDATION

(1919) The brothers form the Mayo Foundation, ensuring the survival of the Mayo Clinic long after their deaths.

Dr. William J. Mayo (l) and Dr. Charles H. Mayo

THE SCIENTISTS

The Mayo Brothers

CHARLES AND WILLIAM MAYO, sons of the surgeon William Worrall Mayo, were raised in Rochester, Minnesota, in an atmosphere heavy with learning. The elder Mayo had come to the United States from Manchester, England, in 1846, and four years later he became a doctor. In 1864 the family moved to Rochester and Mayo set up a small practice.

His two sons, Will and Charlie, were eager to learn about medicine. The boys would go to work with their father and assist him in various capacities, even autopsies. Later they both went to medical school.

In the same year, after a tornado struck Rochester, a group of Catholic nuns joined with the elder Mayo to set up a makeshift hospital to tend to the injured townspeople. In the course of time, funds were raised to establish a permanent facility, and in 1889 the Sisters of St. Francis, along with Mayo and his two sons (now back from medical school), formed a partnership in what became the twenty-seven-bed St. Mary's Hospital. When more space was needed, plans for a new building became a reality and the facility became known as the Mayo Clinic.

The Mayo Clinic soon developed a lofty reputation for care, diagnosis, and clinical research. Specialties were developed, from dietetics to anesthesiology, from surgery to nursing, and as a matter of policy, the results of research were available to any physician who might happen to need them. The clinic's role in educating physicians was formalized in 1915 when the Mayo Foundation for Medical Education and Research was established.

The Mayo brothers died in 1939, just a few months apart. They had formed the Mayo Foundation in 1919, ensuring the survival of the Mayo Clinic long after their deaths. From a local hospital with 27 beds, the Mayo Clinic had by that time become a vast complex with more than 1,000 beds, treating tens of thousands of patients every year.

The Mayo Clinic developed a lofty reputation for care, diagnosis, and clinical research. Specialties were developed, from dietetics to anesthesiology, from surgery to nursing, and as a matter of policy, the results of research were available to any physician who might happen to need them.

PETER AGRE WAS BORN in Northfield, Minnesota, in 1949 and attended Minneapolis Roosevelt High School and Augsburg College, graduating with a B.A. in 1970. From there he went on to Johns Hopkins University School of Medicine, where he obtained his M.D. in 1974, after which he received a fellowship from the University of North Carolina, in Chapel Hill.

Agre returned to Johns Hopkins to teach in 1981. He gained widespread notice in the medical community in 1988 when he successfully isolated a membrane protein. In 1991 it was determined that this membrane protein was the water channel that scientists had long been in search of.

The discovery and isolation of this water channel, or "aquaporin," has had profound significance in the world of biochemical, physiological and genetic studies. Water channels serve a fundamental function in the transport of water in muscle, kidney, and brain tissue. Since Agre's initial discoveries, aquaporins have also be discovered in the eye, and in salivary and tear glands, as well as in mammals, plants, and even bacteria. The malfunctioning of these channels has been associated with several diseases, and scientists are now at work on drugs to combat water-channel defects.

Since 1993 Agre has been professor of biological chemistry at Johns Hopkins School of Medicine. In 2003 the Nobel Prize in chemistry was awarded to Agre, along with Roderick MacKinnon of Rockefeller University, for his discovery of water channels.

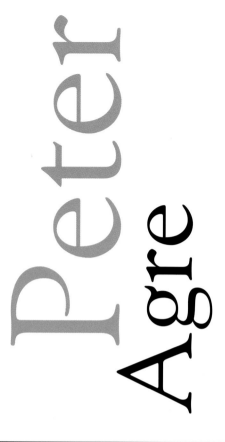

As professor of cell biology at Johns Hopkins University, Agre is awarded the Nobel Prize in Chemistry for his discovery of aquaporins.

C. Walton Lillehei

DR. CLARENCE WALTON LILLEHEI was born in Minneapolis on October 23, 1918. He attended West High School in Minneapolis and graduated from the University of Minnesota in 1939, with the idea of pursuing a career in medicine. Three years later he graduated from the University of Minnesota Medical School.

During World War II Lillehei served in the African and Italian theaters. He returned to the University of Minnesota after the war to complete his training under Dr. Owen Wangensteen. He became an instructor in the Department of Surgery in 1951.

It was during his years at University hospital that Lillehei became the Father of Open-heart Surgery. At the time there was little optimism among surgeons about whether such procedures could be completed successfully without the aid of an artificial heart—still decades away from being workable—but Lillehei developed a technique of cross-circulation to keep patients alive during dangerous and complicated heart operations. Using this technique, Lillehei successfully repaired a ventricular septal defect for the first time, and within the next year more than forty successful open heart surgeries took place. The following year, working with Dr. Richard A. DeWall, Lillehei developed a workable bubble oxegenator to replace the complex and dangerous cross-circulation technique. Four years later he made history once again by using a pacemaker during open-heart surgery for the first time. Lillehei later played a central role in the development of a portable, implantable pacemaker device.

Lillehei continued his devotion to the University of Minnesota Hospital until 1967, when he became the chairman of the Department of Surgery at the Cornell University Major Medical Center and surgeon-in-chief at New York Hospital. He was nominated for the Nobel Prize more than once.

Lillehei stopped performing surgery after he developed cataracts at the age of 55. He returned to the University of Minnesota late in his career to teach once again in the Department of Surgery. In the course of his career he has taught hundreds of cardiothoracic surgeons, many of whom have gone on to head cardiac programs in other parts of the world. Meanwhile, in his laboratories a number of artificial valves were developed that continue to save lives today.

In 1970, Lillehei was appointed director of medical affairs for St. Jude Medical, Incorporated, in St. Paul, a position he held until his death.

Lillehei died on July 5, 1999. His legacy continues at the Lillehei Heart Institute at the University of Minnesota.

Sister Elizabeth
Kenny

ELIZABETH KENNY REVOLUTIONIZED the treatment of poliomyelitis. She was born in New South Wales, Australia, in 1886. She worked as a bush nurse in the Australian outback and served in the navy during World War I.

During her time in the outback, Kenny encountered an epidemic of infantile paralysis. Knowing nothing of the disease, she treated the muscle spasms with warm towels, exercise, and massage and found that her patients were responding to the treatment. When she reported her surprising results, some doctors were encouraged while others began referring to her as a quack. At the time, polio was traditionally treated with braces, splints, and casts to prevent strong muscles from pulling weaker muscles out of position.

In 1933 Kenny established a clinic in Townsville, Australia, dedicated to treating victims of polio by means of the new methods she had devised in the field.

Convinced of the effectiveness of her methods, and inspired by the desire to spread her treatments more widely, Kenny lectured in the United States in the early 1940s—though she often faced resistance from local physicians.

When Kenny met with doctors at the Mayo Clinic in Rochester, they advised her to visit Minneapolis and St. Paul, where there were more cases of polio to be treated. In the Twin Cities she demonstrated her methods to doctors at Gillette and St. Paul Children's hospitals, and they were impressed. Almost overnight doctors gave the order at Gillette and Children's: nurses were to take all restrictive splints and casts off of the patients suffering from polio. From now on the Kenny method would be implemented.

Dr. Wallace Cole at the University of Minnesota Medical School asked Kenny what she needed to stay in Minnesota, and she told him just a meal a day and a bed. So, Kenny began teaching at the University of Minnesota Medical School.

In time she gained the support of the American Medical Association, and in 1943 she set up the Elizabeth Kenny Institute of Minneapolis, Minnesota, to train nurses and physical therapy staff in her treatment methods.

Kenny remained one of the most respected women in America until her death nine years later, finally surpassing Eleanor Roosevelt in a Gallop poll in 1951.

Dr. Wallace Cole at the University of Minnesota Medical School asked Kenny what she needed to stay in Minnesota, and she told him just a meal a day and a bed. So, Kenny began teaching at the University of Minnesota Medical School.

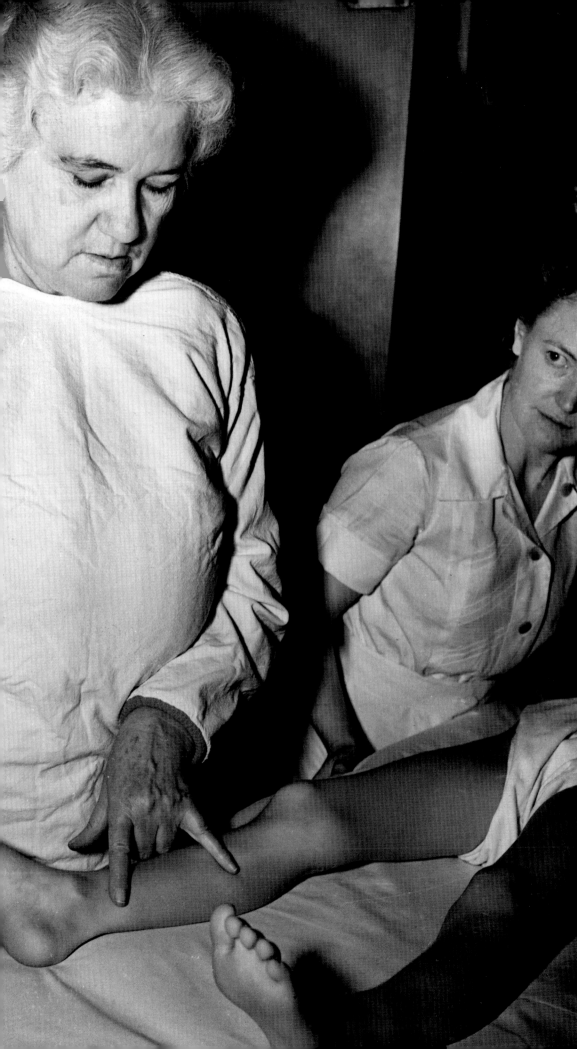

BUSH NURSE

While tending villagers in the Australian outback, Kenny improvises a new method for treating the victims of polio.

UNIVERSITY OF MINNESOTA HOSPITAL

(1940–1942) Dr. Wallace Cole of University Hospital recommends Kenny's services to other physicians: she starts working at area hospitals.

SISTER KENNY INSTITUTE

(1942) Physical therapy has its early beginning at this Minneapolis Clinic, which would become a national leader in the field.

JUST A FAD?

(1944) The National Foundation for Infantile Paralysis calls Kenny's method of treatment a "fad of the moment."

CONTINUING RESEARCH

(1945) The Sister Kenny Foundation is established to distribute research grants and to work with the Minnesota Health Department and the University of Minnesota in developing a live-virus oral polio vaccine.

NORMAN BORLAUG

Norman Borlaug

NORMAN BORLAUG WAS BORN in Cresco, Iowa, on March 25, 1914. He studied forestry at the University of Minnesota, graduating in 1937. Upon graduating he went to work for the U.S. Forestry Service, but he returned to the university to study plant pathology, receiving a master's degree in 1939 and a doctorate in 1942.

After doing research with Du Pont for a few years, Borlaug was appointed director of the Cooperative Wheat Research and Production Program in Mexico. This program, a joint venture of the Rockefeller Foundation and the Mexican government, had as its mission to coordinate research in many related fields—agronomy, genetics, plant breeding, cereal technology, plant pathology, entomology—to develop strains of wheat that would yield more while suffering less from both the preda-

tions of insects and the effects of drought.

In the course of time, Borlaug and his team succeeded in developing new strains of wheat that possessed these qualities. By introducing these new varieties to wide-spread cultivation, yields were increased dramatically not only in Mexico, but also in parts of India and Pakistan, thus lifting millions of farmers out of poverty and alleviating hunger more dramatically than at any previous time in history.

The work spearheaded by Borlaug has been described as the Green Revolution. For his tireless efforts not only to produce new strains of wheat and other grains, but also to train farmers and agricultural advisors throughout the developing world in the wise use and promulgation of such resources, Borlaug was awarded the Nobel Prize in 1970.

Phillip Hench & E.C. Kendall

PHILLIP HENCH AND E.C. KENDALL received the Nobel Prize in Medicine in 1950 for their work on the therapeutic effects of the steroid cortisone.

Born in 1896 in Pittsburgh, Pennsylvania, Hench graduated from Lafayette College in 1916 and went on to earn his M.D. from the University of Pittsburgh Medical School. He later moved to Minnesota to work at the Mayo Clinic in Rochester.

During the 1930s Hench made an extended study of arthritic diseases. He had noticed that both pregnancy and jaundice mitigated the pain associated with arthritis. Eventually he determined that the active agent was a steroid. Another physician at the Mayo Clinic, Dr. E.C. Kendall, had isolated several steroids from the cortex of the adrenal gland. The two doctors eventually decided to test one of these substances, cortisone, on arthritic patients.

Kendall was born on March 8, 1886, in South Norwalk, Connecticut. He received a bachelor's degree in chemistry from Columbia University in 1908 and a doctorate in biochemistry in 1910. Realizing that the surroundings at the Mayo Clinic would be more conducive to his research, he accepted a job offer there in 1914. In subsequent research Kendall succeeded in extracting hormones from the thyroid gland at levels of concentration one hundred times greater than had previously been possible.

For their collaboration on the use of steroids to treat arthritis, Kendall and Hench, along with the Swiss scientist Tadeus Reichstein, were awarded the Nobel Prize.

Phillip Hench (l) and E.C. Kendall

THE WRITERS

F. Scott Fitzgerald

F. SCOTT FITZGERALD was born in St. Paul, Minnesota, on September 24, 1896, and attended St. Paul Academy and a Catholic prep school out East. He went to Princeton University before dropping out to join the army. While stationed in the South, Fitzgerald began writing his first book, *This Side of Paradise* (1920), and it was also there that he met and fell in love with seventeen-year-old Zelda Sayre.

Fitzgerald courted Sayre for several years, but she refused to marry him until he had proved himself as a writer. Eventually some of his short stories were published in the *Saturday Evening Post*. This, along with the publication of *This Side of Paradise*, gave the Fitzgeralds the lifestyle they so desired.

As the decade progressed, Fitzgerald chronicled the lives of glamorous women and men with great success, and before long the couple had become a fixture in elite society. His stories were collected into popular books such as *The Beautiful and the Damned* and *The Jazz Age*, and in 1926 Fitzgerald produced what many consider to be the quintessential American novel, *The Great Gatsby*. The book was not a success at the time, however. It was too sad, too nostalgic, too hopeless for the times.

Meanwhile, the Fitzgeralds moved to Europe, living in France, Italy, and Switzerland—experiences that made their way into Fitzgerald's fourth novel, *Tender is the Night* (1934). By the time it appeared, however, the Depression was well underway, and few readers were inclined to buy a book about rich, self-destructive Americans living on the Riviera. The book was a flop.

High living had begun to take its toll, and Zelda's mental health had deteriorated to the point where she was hospitalized for long stretches of time. Badly in need of funds, in 1937 Fitzgerald signed on with Metro-Goldwyn-Mayer to write movie scripts. He died in Hollywood from a heart attack three years later at the age of forty-four.

In 1926 Fitzgerald produced what many consider to be the quintessential American novel, *The Great Gatsby*. The book was not a success at the time, however. It was too sad, too nostalgic, too hopeless for the times.

BORN ON NOVEMBER 14, 1908, in Minneapolis, Harrison Salisbury graduated from North Side High in 1925, and attended the University of Minnesota, where he became the managing editor of the *Minnesota Daily*. He was expelled from the university for organizing staff members to break the smoking rules of the library, but he was later reinstated and graduated in 1930 with a degree in journalism.

By this time Salisbury had already been working for two years as a reporter for the *Minneapolis Journal*. Upon receiving his degree Salisbury took a job with the St. Paul office of *United Press International (UPI)*, where the story of his campaign in defense of smoking was already well known. (It eventually made the front page of the *New York Times*.)

Salisbury worked up the ladder with *UPI*, first in Chicago, and then in Washington D.C. and New York. In 1942 he was appointed the *UPI* bureau chief in London, and two years later he was sent to Russia to cover the struggles of the Red Army against the Nazis. While behind the iron curtain, Salisbury learned the Russian language by reading *Pravda* every day and working with a tutor.

Following the war, Salisbury returned to an editor's desk in New York. He had wanted to work for the *New York Times*, however, and in 1949 he became their Moscow correspondent. He covered the death of Soviet leader Joseph Stalin in 1953, and he visited the slave labor camps in Siberia, where he feared for his own life. The articles he wrote on Soviet politics and society were given the Pulitzer Prize for International Reporting in 1955.

Salisbury returned to the United States in 1956 to become an editor with the *New York Times*. His incendiary coverage of the civil rights movement led to a $10 million libel suit—later dismissed. He was the first journalist allowed to report from North Vietnam. He was nearly awarded another Pulitzer in 1967 for his interview with North Vietnamese premier Pham Van Dong, who claimed that the success of the U.S. bombing missions had been exaggerated. After a judging committee selected Salisbury as the winner, he was refused the award for political reasons.

In 1970 Salisbury moved to the *OpEd* page of the *Times*, which he edited for five years before retiring from the paper in 1975.

During his very active career, Salisbury also found the time to write two novels and over twenty books on history and current affairs. In later life he continued to write prolifically, and his three volumes of memoirs are widely considered to be a classic account of a reporter's life. He died in 1993.

Harrison Salisbury

Eric Sevareid

ERIC SEVAREID WAS A LEADING foreign correspondent for CBS radio during World War II. Eventually he became part of CBS's *Evening News*.

Sevareid attended Minneapolis Central High School and was editor of the *Central High News*. At the age of eighteen he and a friend canoed to Hudson's Bay, a distance of more than 2,000 miles. His narrative of the trip, *Canoeing with the Cree*, was published five years later.

Sevareid attended the University of Minnesota, where he wrote for the *Minnesota Daily*, and at the same time he worked as a reporter for the *Minneapolis Journal*, though he was fired from that post in 1937 as a result of political disputes with the management. At that point he and his wife Lois packed up and left for France, and along the way they had dinner with an acquaintance named Edwin R. Murrow.

In Paris, Sevareid got work writing and editing, and eventually he became the night editor of the Paris branch of *UPI*. Then he received a fateful call from Murrow, who was building a cadre of young journalists for CBS radio. Sevareid became Murrow's correspondent in France. In fact, he was the last American journalist to leave Paris before the fall of the city, and also the one to break the news from Bordeaux that France had capitulated to the Germans.

In 1941, CBS assigned Sevareid to a news desk in Washington, D.C., and in 1942 he was named head of the Washington bureau. From that point on he held a variety of posts in radio and in television, reporting on events at home and abroad to millions of listeners, until his retirement in 1977.

Sevareid wrote a book describing his experience during World War II, *Not So Wild a Dream* (1946).

HARRISON SALISBURY

UNIVERSITY OF MINNESOTA

(1925–1929) As editor of the campus newspaper the *Minnesota Daily*, Salisbury organizes a protest against the no smoking policy in the library and is expelled; however, he later receives his degree in journalism.

WORLD WAR II JOURNALIST

(1942) He is working for *United Press International* in London and meets Walter Cronkite.

PULITZER PRIZE

(1955) His fourteen-part series on Russia appears in the *New York Times* and Salisbury receives the Pulitzer for international reporting.

EDITOR

(1962) Salisbury becomes the national news editor at the *New York Times*.

ERIC SEVAREID

UNIVERSITY OF MINNESOTA

(1934) Eric Sevareid graduates with a bachelor's degree in political science from the University of Minnesota.

MURROW'S BOYS

(1938) Sevareid goes to work for CBS and Edward Murrow. He is respectfully considered to be one of the Murrow boys.

BOOK PUBLISHED

(1946) *Not So Wild a Dream*, Sevareid's book about his encounters as a journalist, is published by Knopf.

THE CBS EVENING NEWS

(1964–1977) Sevareid is a mainstay on the popular show hosted by Walter Cronkite.

RETIREMENT

(1977) A passing of the torch takes place as one of the Murrow boys leaves the evening news for good.

Garrison Keillor

GARRISON KEILLOR WAS BORN Gary Edward Keillor on August 7, 1942, in Anoka, Minnesota. He was raised in a conservative household where television was forbidden, and drinking, dancing, and singing were frowned upon. As a youth Keillor relied on the radio for entertainment, and the claims it made on his imagination were later to bear fruit in both his writing career and his remarkable success in reviving the tradition of live radio entertainment.

At an early age Keillor developed the habit of reading the *New Yorker*, and as a teen he started his own newspaper, the *Sunnyvale Star*. He attended the University of Minnesota, where he graduated in 1966 with a bachelor's degree in English. As he worked toward his master's degree he held jobs at various radio stations in the Twin Cities and St. Cloud.

In 1969 the *New Yorker* accepted one of Keillor's short stories, and before long his work began appearing in its pages regularly. In 1974, while doing a story in Nashville on the Grand Ole Opry, Keillor conceived the idea of an old-fashioned radio entertainment, and later that year the first broadcast of *A Prairie Home Companion* played to a live audience of twelve people. At first the show was broadcast regionally on Minnesota Public Radio (MPR), but its whimsical combination of jokes, skits, musical performances, imaginary product advertisements, and weekly monologue eventually became so popular that in 1980 the show was picked up nationally and won the George Foster Peabody Broadcasting Award soon afterward.

Keillor published his first collection of short stories, *Happy to Be Here*, in 1982, and three years later the novel *Lake Wobegon Days* appeared. The book was a resounding success, and Keillor was featured on the cover of *Time*, where he was described as "the funniest man in America." *Leaving Home: A Collection of Lake Wobegon Stories*, followed in 1997.

By that time Keillor himself had left both the Twin Cities and *A Prairie Home Companion* behind. After spending a few months in Denmark with his new wife, he moved to New York to become a staff writer for the *New Yorker*. In 1992, however, the *New Yorker* hired a new editor who had little use for Keillor's folksy, down-home charm, and he was let go. Returning to the Twin Cities, he revived *A Prairie Home Companion*, and since that time he has continued to host the popular radio show, which reaches an audience of more than three million people on National Public Radio every Saturday night.

Keillor also continues to write novels and short stories, and he is a frequent contributor to *Time*, *Atlantic Monthly*, and *Salon.com*.

A Prairie Home Companion was broadcast regionally on MPR, and its whimsical combination of jokes, skits, musical performances, and weekly monologue eventually became so popular that in 1980 the show was picked up nationally.

GARRISON KEILLOR

ANOKA

(1942) Gary Edward Keillor is born.

UNIVERSITY OF MINNESOTA

(1966) Keillor graduates with a bachelor's degree in English. He later obtains his master's degree in English there as well.

RADIO SHOW

(1974) *A Prairie Home Companion* airs for the first time. Keillor comes up with the idea for the radio show while writing an article for the *New Yorker* about the Grand Ole Opry.

LAKE WOBEGON DAYS

(1985) The novel about a Minnesota boy with a strict Lutheran upbringing becomes a best seller.

RETURN OF A PRAIRIE HOME COMPANION

(1993) After several years of being broadcast from New York as the *American Radio Company*, the popular radio show returns to downtown St. Paul.

John Sanford

JOHN CAMP USED TO ATTEND crime scenes as a news reporter for the *Pioneer Press*. In his novels, written under the pseudonym John Sanford, he writes bone-chilling descriptions of murders, often committed in the Twin Cities area.

Camp was born in Cedar Rapids, Iowa, on February 23, 1944. He is a graduate of University of Iowa. After college, he joined the army and was stationed in Korea, where he wrote for a military newspaper. After returning from the service he obtained his master's degree in journalism.

From 1970 to 1978, Camp worked for the *Miami Herald*. In 1978 he went to work for the *St. Paul Pioneer Press and Dispatch*, first as a general reporter and later as a featured columnist. His five-part series in 1986 titled "Life on the Land: An American Farm Family" won a Pulitzer Prize. A year later his first novel was published under the name John Sanford. Since then he has written a long string of best sellers detailing the career of St. Paul police detective Lucas Davenport. The book *Naked Prey* (2003) reached Number One on the *New York Times* best seller list.

Jon Hassler

JON HASSLER HAS WRITTEN a number of popular novels rooted in his experience of small-town Minnesota life.

He was born in Minneapolis on April 30, 1933, but raised in Staples, where his father ran a grocery store, and later in Plainview. He attended St. John's University in College-ville and received his master's degree from the University of North Dakota. He spent the next ten years teaching high school English and then joined the faculty at Bemidji Sate University.

Hassler began writing fiction seriously in 1970. His first novel, *Staggerford*, was published in 1977. Since that time, new works have appeared at fairly regular intervals, as Hassler explores a world of characters and situations drawn from small-town and campus life. His works include *Simon's Night* (1979), *The Love Hunter* (1981), *A Green Journey* (1985), and *Rookery Blues* (1995).

Although Hassler's style has remained traditional, he makes effective use of letters, journal entries, and flashbacks to expose subtle nuances of feeling within and between his characters. The characters themselves are drawn from many walks of life, and the success with which Hassler almost invariably brings them to life is a mark of his deep affection for both the foibles and the idiosyncrasies of the ordinary men and women that make up our world.

In 1980 Hassler was appointed writer-in-residence at St. John's University; in 1988 CBS aired an adaptation of *A Green Journey* starring Angela Lansbury and Denholm Elliott.

Robert Bly

ROBERT BLY

BIRTH

(1926) Robert Bly is born on December 23, 1926, in Madison, Minnesota.

COLLEGE

(1946–1950) Bly attends St. Olaf College for a year, transfers to Harvard, and becomes the literary editor of the *Harvard Advocate*; he would bring in Don Hall, and later John Ashbery.

POLITICAL ACTIVIST

(1966) Bly cofounds American Writers Against the Vietnam War.

IRON JOHN: A BOOK ABOUT MEN

(1990) Bly writes a book about how men should deal with their manhood, using a mythical figure from a Grimm fairy tale.

EDITOR

Bly helps to expose readers to world poetry with three popular anthologies, *News of the Universe* (1980), *The Rag and Bone Shop of the Heart* (1992), and *The Soul Is Here for Its Own Joy* (1995).

ROBERT BLY WAS BORN on December 23, 1926, in Madison, Minnesota, and raised on a nearby farm. He spent two years in the navy during World War II and later attended St. Olaf College with ambitions of becoming a doctor. One year later, however, he left to study literature at Harvard, where he found himself in the company of other young and aspiring poets such as Adrienne Rich, Kenneth Koch, John Ashbery, Harold Brodky, John Hawkes, and Donald Hall.

Bly graduated magna cum laude from Harvard with a bachelor's degree in 1950, but the next few years were rough. He lived in Manhattan, wrote, studied, and did all manner of odd jobs to scrape by. He returned to the Midwest in 1954, to the Iowa Writer's Workshop, where he earned his master's two years later. The following year he went to Norway on a Fulbright scholarship, and it was here that he began his lifelong exploration of poetry from other nations.

On his return to the United States, Bly moved to a farm in western Minnesota and began to publish the influential journal *The Fifties* (later *The Sixties*, and then *The Seventies*), in which Pablo Neruda, Georg Trakl, Cesar Vallejo, Gunnar Ekelof, Harry Martinson, and other outstanding foreign poets were introduced to a wider American audience.

During the 1960s, Bly became a leader in the movement against American involvement in the Vietnam War. His poetry became more topical, but without losing the haunting depth and personal flavor he had developed during his long apprenticeship. When *The Light Around the Body* won the National Book Award in 1968, he donated the prize money to the resistance.

Bly's career took a new turn with the publication of *Iron John* in 1991. It reached the top of the best-seller list, was translated into many languages, and thrust Bly into the forefront of what became known as the "men's movement." The book had the unusual merit of relating the mythic underworld of the psyche to engaging social issues of the day by means of common language.

Since that time, Bly has frequently conducted workshops along with James Hillman, Marian Woodman, and other colleagues, while continuing to publish the poems that make him one of the literary luminaries of our time.

LOUISE ERDRICH WAS BORN in Little Falls, Minnesota, in 1954, the daughter of a French Ojibwe mother and a German American father. A member of the Turtle Mountain Band of Ojibwe Indians, Erdrich was raised on the Wahpeton Indian Reservation in North Dakota, where her parents worked. Her father encouraged her literary aspirations from an early age by giving her a nickel for every story she wrote. She entered the Dartmouth Native American Studies Program in 1972, later earned a master's degree at John Hopkins, and became writer-in-residence at Dartmouth in 1981, where she married Michael Dorris, the director of Dartmouth's Native American Studies Program.

In 1982, Erdrich's short story, "The World's Greatest Fisherman," won the Nelson Algren fiction competition. The story later became the opening chapter of her first novel, *Love Medicine*. The novel was highly acclaimed and won the National Book Critics Circle Award for 1984. Erdrich went on to write *The Beet Queen*, *Tracks*, *The Bingo Palace*, and *Tales of Burning Love*, all of which share the same cast of characters and a roving and imaginative sense of present and past time.

Over the years Erdrich's stories have appeared in many magazines, including the *New Yorker*, *Ms.*, and *Harper's*. She has been awarded the Pushcart Prize for poetry, the O. Henry Prize for short fiction, the Western Literary Association Award, and a Guggenheim fellowship. A mother of five children, Erdrich has also written several children's books, as well as a book about the experience of raising an infant.

Erdrich's father encouraged her to write from an early age by giving her a nickel for every story she wrote.

August Wilson

FREDERICK AUGUST KITTEL was born on April 27, 1945, in Pittsburgh, Pennsylvania. The family of six lived in a two-bedroom apartment in the Hill District, a poor neighborhood. Wilson later moved to the white suburb of Hazelwood, where he was called nigger by some of his classmates. When a teacher accused him unjustly of plagiarism, Wilson abruptly dropped out of school and began going to the local public library to read on his own.

Wilson's mother wanted August to become an attorney, but the young man chose to become a writer instead. He worked to support himself as a busboy, a stock boy, and a mailroom clerk for nearly fifteen years before his efforts began to bear fruit. While in Pittsburgh he even founded a theater company, Black Horizons on the Hill.

Wilson moved to St. Paul, Minnesota, in 1978, and it was here that he began to develop the sensitivity to black vernacular speech that would later make him famous. Wilson had come to St. Paul to visit a friend, Charles Purdy, with whom he had worked in Pittsburgh. Purdy had by now become the director of St. Paul's Penumbra Theatre. Before long Wilson was living in St. Paul and writing scripts for the Science Museum of Minnesota. Some of the more notable scripts he wrote are "An Evening with Margaret Mead," "How Coyote Got His Special Power and Used It to Help the People," and "Eskimo Song Duel."

In 1980 Wilson's play *Jitney* was accepted by the Minneapolis Playwright's Center, and Wilson was named an associate playwright. In *Jitney*, for the first time, Wilson showed his signature talent of using authentic black speech to extraordinary dramatic affect. In the same vein, he wrote *Ma Rainey's Black Bottom* in 1982. This play impressed Lloyd Richards of the prestigious Yale Repertory Theater, and after two years of rewriting, it was performed at Yale to rave reviews. It opened later that year at the Cort Theatre on Broadway and was voted Best Play of the Year (1984–85) by the New York Drama Critics' Circle.

By this time Wilson had embarked on the ambitious project of writing a ten-play cycle about the African-American experience, with each play focused on a different decade. Wilson's play *Fences* became his biggest success. Opening on Broadway in March 1987, it won the Pulitzer Prize for Best Drama. He won another Pulitzer for the 1990 Broadway play *The Piano Lesson*. Other well-known plays in the cycle include *Joe Turner's Come and Gone* and *Two Trains Running*.

SINCLAIR LEWIS WAS BORN in 1885 in Sauk Centre, Minnesota. The son of a country doctor, he attended Yale University and wrote for the *Yale Literary Review*. After college he became a newspaper reporter, and for the next five years Lewis took various jobs editing and writing book reviews, while honing his own writing at night. His fiction was eventually published in magazines, and the first of many novels appeared after World War I.

Lewis was an established, if little-known, novelist when *Main Street* was published in 1920. Readers throughout the United States were astounded by the blend of satire and realism Lewis had brought to his portrait of a fictional Midwest town called Gopher Prairie, and to the young woman who struggles to escape its provincialism and dolor. Critics praised its sensitive handling of vernacular language and its absorbing depictions of everyday life. On the other hand, many Minnesotans, especially those living in Sauk Centre, took the book personally and chastised Lewis for writing it.

With his next book, *Babbitt* (1922), Lewis offered the reader a far more interesting creation. A portrait of a pragmatic American businessman, *Babbitt* possesses many technical virtues that *Main Street* lacks, and remains today Lewis's most readable novel.

Lewis's next work, *Arrowsmith* (1925), played on similar themes of midwestern small-mindedness and cultural poverty. It was awarded the Pulitzer Prize, but Lewis refused the award, noting that its purpose was to honor an outstanding presentation of "the wholesome atmosphere of American life," which *Arrowsmith* definitely was not. He continued his string of successes with *Dodsworth* (1929), and the next year he became the first American recipient of the Nobel Prize for Literature.

Although Lewis continued to write and publish for two decades, his creative spark had dimmed. He expanded his themes to include fascism, racism, religious fanaticism, and hypocritical philanthropy, but his writing had become dull and his analysis superficial.

Lewis died in Rome in 1951.

Sinclair Lewis

Thomas Friedman

CONSIDERED BY MANY to be one of the foremost experts on the Middle East, Thomas Friedman has won the Pulitzer Prize three times for his writings on the volatile region.

Friedman was born in Minneapolis, Minnesota, on July 20, 1953, and grew up in St. Louis Park. He received his bachelor's degree in Mediterranean studies from Brandeis University in 1975. From there, he attended St. Anthony's College in Oxford on a Marshall Scholarship. In 1978 he received his master of philosophy degree in modern Eastern studies from Oxford.

A reporter with the *New York Times* since 1981 and the foreign affairs columnist on the *OpEd* page since 1995, Friedman won the Pulitzer in 1983 for his coverage of the Israeli invasion of Beirut. In 1988 he was given the award again for his fair and accurate coverage of Israeli affairs; and for a third time in 2002 for his commentary on the terrorist attacks on the World Trade Center and Pentagon.

Friedman has appeared on many television programs since the September 11 attacks, including *The Late Show* with David Letterman (CBS), *Meet the Press* (NBC), and *Face the Nation* (CBS). He is also the author of several books, including *From Beirut to Jerusalem* (1989), for which he won the National Book Award for nonfiction in 1989; *Israel: A Photobiography* (1998); *The Lexus and the Olive Tree: Understanding Globalization* (1999); and *The World Is Flat* (2005).

Ole E. Rølvaag

IN HIS BOOK *Giants in the Earth* (1927), Rølvaag wonderfully depicts the lifestyle of Norwegians in 1870 Dakota.

Rølvaag was born on Donna Island, Norway, on April 22, 1876. He worked as a fisherman before emigrating to the United States in 1896, where he attended Augustana Academy in South Dakota, and then St. Olaf College, in Northfield, Minnesota. Rølvaag graduated in 1905 and considered doing graduate work at Harvard, but decided in the end to accept a position at St. Olaf teaching Norwegian language, literature, and history.

Rølvaag became a fixture at St. Olaf over the years, but his greater contribution to the area came about as a result of his activities as a novelist.

Rølvaag wrote and published in Norwegian about the immigrant experience with insight and compassion, and he also closely supervised the translation of many of his works into English. In the course of time, he produced a series of novels that includes *The Boat of Longing*, *Peder Victorious*, and *Their Father's Gold*. But his crowning achievement was *Giants in the Earth*, which, in the English translation, has never been out of print since its appearance in 1927. In *Giants in the Earth* Rølvaag captured, perhaps better than anyone before or since, the lives of those immigrants who, cut off from their native traditions, settled the bounteous but also harsh and desolate region of the American prairies.

John Berryman

JOHN BERRYMAN'S COLLECTION of poems *The Dream Songs*, has been called the most heroic work in American poetry since World War II.

Berryman was born on October 25, 1914, in McAlester, Oklahoma. His father was a banker and petty land speculator, and the family moved from town to town frequently. In 1925, following a series of financial setbacks, Berryman's parents separated, and a year later, when he was eleven, his father committed suicide. This dark event left a wound on Berryman's psyche that never healed.

Not long afterward Berryman's mother married a bond broker, the family moved to New York, and John was sent off to a boarding school in Connecticut. Four years later he entered Columbia University, where Mark Van Doren took the talented young scholar under his wing. Berryman excelled at Columbia, won several poetry prizes, and eventually received a fellowship to Cambridge.

In the course of the 1940s, Berryman received appointments at several distinguished East Coast universities, and in 1942 he published his first book of poems. But as his reputation grew, his health began to decline; his battle with alcoholism began increasingly to undermine both his professionalism and his family life, and he was hospitalized several times for exhaustion.

In 1955 Berryman was appointed to a teaching post at the University of Minnesota, and he continued to teach there until his death seventeen years later. It was during his years in Minnesota that Berryman's poetry shed the last vestiges of derivative literary influence, and he began to fully exploit the fractured syntax and chaotic emotionalism characteristic of his mature style. Beginning with *Homage to Mistress Bradstreet* in 1956, he produced a succession of fine works upon which his fame as a poet largely rests. His collection *77 Dream Songs* (1964), won the Pulitzer Prize; two years later *Early Poems* and *Sonnets* appeared. That same year he was awarded prizes from the Academy of American Poets and the National Endowment for the Arts. The second installment of the Dream Songs, entitled *His Toy, His Dream, His Rest,* won a National Book Award in 1969.

But the honors he was receiving did nothing to arrest Berryman's slide into extreme alcoholism, and in 1970 he was hospitalized for five months. His collection of autobiographical poems, *Love & Fame*, appeared the same year, oddly exhibiting a newfound stylistic clarity and calm. It also contained a humorous yet sincere section entitled "Eleven Addresses to the Lord": In his efforts to get a grip on himself, Berryman had turned to religion.

Berryman continued to teach and write, but in the end he could not tame his demons, and on January 7, 1972, he jumped to his death from the Washington Avenue Bridge in Minneapolis.

Sigurd Olson

SIGURD OLSON WAS BORN in Chicago, Illinois, in 1899, but spent much of his childhood in northern Wisconsin, where he developed a love of the north woods that inspired him throughout his career as an author, educator, and environmentalist. He graduated from the University of Wisconsin in 1920 and taught biology at Ely Junior College from 1922 to 1935. During this time he also travelled widely and guided in the Quetico-Superior region along the Minnesota-Ontario border, which was then a sprawling but unprotected expanse of dazzling lakes and dense pine forests.

Olson expressed his love of the region in essays and reflections, many of which appeared in a series of popular books. In 1974 he received the Burroughs Medal, the highest honor in nature writing, for *Wilderness Days* (1972). His other books include *Listening Point* (1958), *The Lonely Land* (1961), *Runes of the North* (1963), *Open Horizons* (1969), and *The Hidden Forest* (1969).

Olson knew that the woodlands surrounding Ely were under assault by lumber, mining, and indiscriminate recreational interests, and he worked tirelessly to preserve the area's pristine character. He fought during the 1920s to keep unnecessary roads and dams out of the Quetico-Superior, and during the 1940s he worked to ban airplanes from flying into the area. Olson served as wilderness ecologist for the Izaak Walton League of America from 1948 until his death in 1982, and he was also elected to high office in the National Parks Association and the Wilderness Society. His crowning achievement may have been his contribution to drafting the Wilderness Act, which became law in 1964 and established the U.S. wilderness preservation system.

In recognition of his unparalleled efforts both to celebrate and to preserve the wilderness, the Izaak Walton League, the Sierra Club, the National Wildlife Federation, and the Wilderness Society have all given Olson their highest award.

CURT CARLSON

SOUTH MINNEAPOLIS YOUTH

(1920s) An industrious boy, Curt Carlson delivers newspapers and works at his father's grocery store on Forty-fourth Street and France Avenue.

UNIVERSITY OF MINNESOTA

(1937) After paying his way through college, Carlson graduates with a degree in economics.

GOLD BOND STAMP COMPANY

(1938) In a festive opening the Gold Bond Stamp is introduced by Carlson at a grocery store on 12th Avenue in Minneapolis.

RADISSON

(1960) The risky purchase of the downtown Minneapolis hotel is a sign of things to come. Carlson Companies would become a huge conglomerate, specializing in the service industries of travel and leisure.

CARLSON SCHOOL OF MANAGEMENT

(1997) The new graduate school of business building at the University of Minnesota opens. Over time Carlson donates almost $50 million to various university programs.

THE BUSINESS LEADERS

Curt Carlson

CURT CARLSON GREW UP in South Minneapolis near his father's grocery store at Forty-fourth Street and France Avenue. His entrepreneurial flair revealed itself early, when, at the age of eleven, he organized a network of paperboys in his neighborhood. After graduating from Minneapolis West High School and the University of Minnesota, Carlson started selling for Procter and Gamble. He was looking for a business opportunity when he and his wife, Arleen, found out about an incentive program at Leader Department Store in Minneapolis, whereby customers received stamps when they purchased items from the store, which they could later redeem for rewards.

Carlson decided to make use of the same promotional device at grocery stores, and in the spring of 1938 his new company, Gold Bond Stamps, introduced the stamps at a grocery store on Twelfth Avenue in Minneapolis. Twenty years later the stamps were in Safeway grocery stores throughout the western United States, and total sales were just under $50 million.

As the sale of Gold Bond Stamps leveled off in the 1960s, Carlson began to diversify his holdings. His acquisition of the Radisson Hotel in downtown Minneapolis was the first of many forays into the hospitality industry, which in time led to the formation of seventy-five separate corporations, including TGI Friday's and Carlson Wagonlit Travel, with total sales of more than $20 billion.

With his donation of $25 million to the University of Minnesota Business School, the school's name was changed to the Carlson School of Management. The doors to the new building were opened in 1997.

Carlson died in 1999. His daughter, Marilyn Nelson, who had been vice chairperson of the board since 1994, was named the president and chief executive officer shortly before her father's death.

> With his donation of $25 million to the University of Minnesota Business School, the school's name was changed to the Carlson School of Management. The doors to the new building were opened in 1997.

WRIGHT WAS THE CHIEF OPERATING OFFICER of Super Valu, Inc. for nearly 20 years. Considered to be a role model for company executives, Wright credits playing football as a contributing factor toward his success in the corporate world.

Wright, who was raised in South Minneapolis, became one of the greatest prep athletes in state history. He attended St. Thomas Academy and the University of Minnesota, where he was captain of the Gopher football team in 1959. Wright was drafted by Vince Lombardi and the Green Bay Packers. Instead he chose to play for the Winnipeg Blue Bombers and coach Bud Grant. Wright played with the Bombers for two seasons, receiving All-Pro honors as a defensive tackle, and his team won the Grey Cup.

Wright returned to school, graduating with honors from the University of Minnesota Law School, and joined the law firm of Dorsey and Whitney in the fall of 1963. After this he fulfilled an ROTC obligation and served in the army from 1964–1966. Wright later returned to Dorsey and Whitney, and in 1969 was made a partner in the firm, which specializes in corporate, tax, and securities law.

Wright made the move to Super Valu, a wholesale food distributor based in Eden Prairie, Minnesota, in 1977, accepting a position as senior vice president. At the time Super Valu sales were $2.5 billion. Before long Wright had been named president and chief operating officer. Under his leadership the company's sales grew to $23 billion. Upon his retirement in 2001, Super Valu employed 65,000 people. It was the fifth-largest grocery store company in the United States, owning and operating not only Cub Foods but also supplying competitors such as Lunds, Kowalski's, Byerly's, and Super Target.

In 1985 Wright was a founding member of the Food Industry Crusade Against Hunger (FICAH), an organization working to give people in underdeveloped areas the skills and resources needed to produce their own food. He has also helped to raise funds for the Food for All program to alleviate hunger in the United States, and he has donated generously to these and other causes through his own company. In 2002 Wright received the Sidney R. Rabb Award, given annually to a single individual who has given a lifetime of exemplary service to the grocery industry.

Mike Wright

Glen Taylor

GLEN TAYLOR, WHO WAS recently listed among the 400 wealthiest Americans by *Forbes Magazine*, was born on April 20, 1941 in Springfield, Minnesota. He grew up on a farm five miles outside of the town of Comfry, where his parents grew alfalfa, corn, and soybeans on 160 acres of rented land. They also raised hogs, cows, sheep, and chicken.

Taylor was very athletic, and he participated in football, basketball, baseball, and track until his senior year in high school. While still in high school, Taylor married a girl from a nearby farm and they had a daughter together.

After graduation, Taylor, his wife Glenda, and their baby daughter moved to Mankato, where he attended Mankato State University while working parttime at Carlson Wedding Service, a specialty printing company. In time Taylor worked his way up the small company, doing a variety of jobs, and he liked the firm so well that upon graduation from Mankato State, he began to look for a teaching position only reluctantly. He would rather have stayed at Carlson, and when they offered him a salary of $4,200 to stay, Taylor took it.

Taylor soon became a manager at Carlson, responsible for inventories, purchasing, and some of the marketing. He also convinced owner Bill Carlson to add more products. In those days wedding invitations were almost always on ivory paper; Taylor suggested they start using different colors and different texts. Reply cards and thank-you notes were also added to the product line.

In 1967 Carlson decided to sell shares to Taylor and two other employees, Jim Holland and Merlyn Anderson; and when Carlson retired in 1974, he sold his majority interest to Taylor. Holland and Anderson agreed to stay on with the company. Both of them were comfortable with Taylor in charge, and when they decided to sell a portion of their minority shares to him, he formed his own holding company, Taylor Corporation, making Carlson Craft the first subsidiary. As opportunities arose Taylor began purchasing other printing companies, and before long he had built an impressive business conglomerate without going into debt.

In 1980 Taylor stepped aside from day-to-day operations, giving his managers the opportunity to show what they could do, and entered the political arena. He served in the state senate from 1980 to 1986. During those years Taylor kept his business out of the senate, and was in fact an extremely dedicated public servant.

After leaving the senate, Taylor's corporation once again became his main focus. It would eventually become a $2 billion corporation, with more than seventy companies located in seventeen states, Canada, the United Kingdom, Australia, the Netherlands, Mexico, and Sweden.

In 1994 Taylor added another dimension to his life, when he purchased the Minnesota Timberwolves basketball team. Within a year he had hired Kevin McHale as his assistant general manager and Flip Saunders as the head coach: both had played college basketball at the University of Minnesota. Taylor and his new team made the news by drafting Kevin Garnett straight out of high school in 1995. Garnett has remained with the Timberwolves ever since, and in 2004 he was named the Most Valuable Player of the National Basketball Association.

EARL BAKKEN WAS PASSIONATE about the story of Frankenstein and the role played by a jolt of electricity in bringing the monster back to life.

Bakken was raised in Minneapolis, attended Columbia Heights High School, and graduated from the University of Minnesota in 1948 with a degree in engineering. The next year, along with Palmer J. Hermundslie, he founded Medtronic, a company that repaired medical devices. In the course of his work Bakken got to know the doctors and nurses at the University of Minnesota Hospital, and in 1957, at the request of Dr. C. Walton Lillehei, a renowned heart surgeon, he created a device to stimulate the human heart. The battery-powered, transistorized device was, in fact, the first pacemaker.

Medtronic soon began manufacturing and distributing its pacemaker widely, and the company grew rapidly. It has long since become the largest and most innovative medical device company in the world, with markets in 120 countries.

Bakken had long been interested in the history of the field in which he worked, and in 1975 he founded the Bakken Library and Museum on the shores of Lake Calhoun to house his extraordinary collection of books relating to the subject of electricity in medicine, and to exhibit his collection of antique medical and electrical devices.

Earl Bakken

At the request of Dr. C. Walton Lillehei, a renowned heart surgeon, Bakken created a device to stimulate the human heart. The battery-powered, transistorized device was, in fact, the first pacemaker.

Rose Totino

ROSE TOTINO, THE DAUGHTER of Italian immigrants, was born in Northeast Minneapolis in 1915. As a child she learned how to cook pizza and pasta standing at her mother's side in the kitchen. She quit school and went to work in a candy factory at age sixteen to bring in more money for the struggling family, and she later married a local baker named Jim Totino.

The young couple was active in the community, and the Totino home soon became a favorite place for gatherings, famous for the wonderful pizza and pasta Rose and Jim prepared. Encouraged by their friends, Rose and Jim took out a loan and opened a shop. As the take-out business grew, they set up tables and opened a restaurant. One thing led to another, and in 1961 Rose and her husband purchased a frozen-food plant. Though there were rocky patches along the road to success, pizza was a relatively new product at the time, and Totino's Pizza became so popular that within ten years the Totinos built a $2.5 million plant in Fridley, Minnesota. In 1975, with annual sales of more than $35 million a year, they sold the business to the Pillsbury company, and Rose became a corporate vice president.

Throughout the long development of her business, Rose emphasized the importance of strong personal relations with both her employees and her customers. As success came her way, she shared it liberally with the community. The Totinos founded a charitable organization, funded local teams, and contributed to many colleges, schools, and community building projects in the area. In recognition of her many donations, in 1980 Grace High School in Fridley changed its name to Totino-Grace High School. Totino died in 1994.

As success came her way, Totino shared it liberally with the community. The Totinos founded a charitable organization, funded local teams, and contributed to many colleges, schools, and community building projects in the area.

Frederick Weyerhaeuser

BORN IN NIEDERSAULHEIM, Germany, in 1834, Frederick Weyerhaeuser immigrated to the United States in 1852, working as a day-laborer, first in Erie, Pennsylvania, and then in Rock Island, Illinois. An indefatigable worker, he eventually drew notice, and was put in charge of a sawmill and timber yard. During one of the industry's frequent bust periods he bought both ventures with money he had saved over the years, and before long he was acquiring tracts of forestland in Wisconsin, Minnesota, Idaho, and the Northwest Coast.

Following the forests west, Weyerhaeuser moved to St. Paul in 1891, where he befriended James J. Hill. Unfamiliar with the lumber business, Hill sold Weyerhaeuser millions of acres at bargain prices. The Weyerhaeuser Corporation was formed shortly thereafter and went on to become a major force in the timber industry.

After Weyerhaeuser's death in 1914 his company continued to prosper. Today the Weyerhaeuser Corporation remains the number-one producer of market pulp and softwood timber in the world. The company employs more than 35,000 people and is headquartered in Tacoma, Washington.

George Draper Dayton

IN 1902 GEORGE DRAPER DAYTON, a banker and real estate broker from Worthington, Minnesota, opened a dry goods store at Seventh and Nicollet in downtown Minneapolis. The store soon developed a reputation for quality merchandise, excellent customer service, and honest advertising. In time, on the strength of these attributes, Dayton and his family built one of America's premier retail chains. George Dayton also founded the Dayton Foundation in 1918, which has contributed greatly over the decades to improving the social fabric of the communities in which Dayton's operates.

Dayton eventually turned the company over to his sons Draper and Nelson, who in turn passed it on to five grandsons, Donald, Douglas, Wallace, Bruce, and Kenneth. The boys continued their grandfather's legacy. In 1956, they built the first indoor shopping mall in the world, Southdale Center in Edina. Less than five years later, in 1962, the first Target store opened in Roseville. Dayton's merged with R L Hudson of Michigan in 1969. Hudson already had seventeen department stores in the upper Midwest. With the acquisition of Marshall Field's of Chicago in the early 1990s, the Dayton Hudson Company expanded considerably more, and in 2000 the company became the Target Corporation.

Target Corporation is often referred to as one of the best-run companies in America.

James J. Hill

JAMES J. HILL

BIRTHPLACE

(1836) James J. Hill is born in Ontario, Canada.

ST. PAUL

(1856) After finding work in St. Paul as a clerk on the levee, the twenty-year-old immigrant spends most of his next twenty years employed in the shipping industry.

RAILWAY PURCHASE

(1878) Hill buys the nearly bankrupt St. Paul and Pacific Railway and sets his sights on taking the rails north to Winnipeg and west to the Pacific Ocean.

THE GREAT NORTHERN

(1890) Renamed the Great Northern, the railway becomes one of the biggest railroads in the world.

DEATH OF THE EMPIRE BUILDER

(1916) Hill dies at his Summit Avenue mansion in St. Paul.

BORN IN ROCKWOOD, ONTARIO, James J. Hill arrived in St. Paul in 1856, at the age of 20, intent on becoming a fur trapper. The last trapping parties had already left for the season, however, so Hill began working as a clerk and freight agent for a line of Mississippi steamboats.

After the Civil War Hill became an agent for the St. Paul and Pacific Railroad. He also sold coal to the rail line to replace the less efficient wood they had been burning. As a result of the experience he gained working for and with the St. Paul and Pacific, Hill identified a need to improve and expand service in the Red River Valley, and to that end he formed a steamship company, The Red River Transportation Company, with Norman Kittson of the Hudson's Bay Company. After the Panic of 1873, the St. Paul and Pacific, which had long been struggling, fell into receivership, and Hill saw his chance to purchase it outright. With the help of Kittson and other Hudson's Bay Company executives, he bought the line for 20 percent of its value, and his career as the Empire Builder began.

Good grain harvests, a flood of new immigrants from Scandinavia, and the timely receipt of a two-million-acre land grant from the government, allowed Hill to realize his dream of returning the St. Paul and Pacific to health, and he was soon envisioning a rail line extending across the northern states to the West Coast. Though often referred to at the time as Hill's Folly, the Great Northern Railroad did eventually reach Puget Sound, due in large part to Hill's personal involvement in every aspect of engineering and route selection. Hill also devised many strategies for enticing settlers to the lands through which his railroads passed, and he engaged in numerous battles with other rail barons on the West Coast.

It would be difficult to exaggerate Hill's contribution to the settling of the northern plains. He died in his Summit Avenue mansion on May 29, 1916.

William Norris

WILLIAM NORRIS PLAYED a central role in the growth of the technology industry in Minnesota. He was born in Nebraska and grew up on a farm. He attended the University of Nebraska, graduating in 1932, after which he went into sales.

During World War II Norris joined the Naval Reserves and was assigned to Washington, D.C. He was successful in code-breaking operations. After the war he went to work for Engineering Research Associates in St. Paul. He left ERA in 1957 to help found Control Data Corporation.

The company set up shop in a warehouse in downtown Minneapolis. Employees Seymour Cray and Jim Thornton designed the fastest computer in the world, and Control Data became respected by its competitors. Over time Norris built Control Data into a huge business conglomerate, at times making joint ventures and friendly takeovers work to his advantage.

During the mid-1960s a new office complex in Bloomington became the headquarters for the rapidly expanding company. In addition to computer services, data services, peripherals discs and tape drives for computers, the company nurtured a social conscience. After race riots in Minneapolis in 1967, Norris assigned deputy chairman Norbert Berg to see what could be done to break down racial barriers. On the strength of Berg's recommendations, Control Data built a plant in the Selby-Dale area in St. Paul. Norris also advanced programs on education, employment, and housing through such organizations as Plato, Control Data Temps, Rural Ventures, and City Ventures.

Meanwhile, Control Data became a leader in the peripherals industry garnering 80 percent of the market. The company had more than 50,000 employees and revenues in excess of $4 billion. Norris even authored a book, *New Frontiers for Business Leadership*, which was published in 1983.

In time the offshore manufacturing of peripherals and the coming of age of the personal computer led to the demise of Control Data. Norris retired in 1986, and five years later he resigned from the board. The company became two separate operations in 1991 with the formation of Ceridian Corporation and Control Data Systems.

In the course of Control Data's long life, former employees have established dozens of new technology companies in the region. The William C. Norris Institute was founded in 1988, (and transferred to the University of St. Thomas in 2001), to stimulate entrepreneurial activity by providing seed capital for endeavors in the technology sector that create jobs for underemployed and unemployed workers.

(1907) McKnight joins the company as an assistant bookkeeper.

ORDWAY CONNECTION

WILLIAM MCKNIGHT WAS BORN in White, South Dakota, on November 11, 1887. He attended the University of Duluth School of Business for a short time before accepting a bookkeeping job with Minnesota Mining and Manufacturing (3M) in 1907. At that time 3M was a struggling start-up company selling an inferior brand of sandpaper. In his capacity as sales manager, McKnight emphasized the importance of listening to the criticisms of the working people who actually used the products he was selling, and as a result he established a small laboratory to monitor quality control and develop new products. Later, as general manager of the firm, McKnight's open-mindedness and eagerness to listen to the customers was matched by the free reign he often gave his chemists and engineers to pursue new lines of development. "Listen to anyone with an idea," was his motto, and in time 3M became synonymous with such popular materials as masking tape, cellophane tape, reflective paint, Post-it notes, and many industrial products.

McKnight died in 1978, but the company he created continues to operate along the lines he initiated. For his distinctive style of management and his remarkable success at transforming a floundering sandpaper company into a world manufacturing leader, *Fortune Magazine* recently included McKnight among a list of the ten greatest CEOs of the twentieth century.

"Listen to anyone with an idea," was McKnight's motto, and in time 3M became synonymous with such popular materials as masking tape, cellophane tape, reflective paint, Post-it notes, and many industrial products.

William McKnight

I. A. O'Shaughnessy

IGNATIUS ALOYSIUS O'Shaughnessy, a wealthy oilman, donated much of his fortune to the construction of buildings that would bear his name.

O'Shaughnessy was born in Stillwater, Minnesota, on July 31, 1885. He studied at the University of St. Thomas, graduating in 1907, and then joined his brother in the insurance business. He soon tired of this pursuit, however, and moved to Blackwell, Oklahoma, to engage in wildcat oil explorations. He struck oil with his first well, and he never looked back.

In 1917 O'Shaughnessy founded Globe Oil and Refining Company of Oklahoma. A four-inch pipeline was laid from the Blackwell field to a newly built refining plant, and oil was refined there for the first time on February 22, 1918. Similar successes in Kansas led to the formation of the Lorio Oil and Gas Company in 1927. A year later O'Shaughnessy incorporated his ven-

tures in Delaware, and began refining oil for Shell and Phillips Petroleum. By 1934 his operation was considered the largest in the world owned by a single individual.

The I. A. O'Shaughnessy Foundation was started in 1941, in St. Paul, Minnesota, and over the years the former wildcatter donated millions of dollars toward the construction of buildings, most notably the football stadium at the University of St. Thomas, the auditorium at the College of St. Catherine, the education center at the University of St. Thomas, and a new St. Thomas Academy High School in Mendota Heights. In recognition of these and other gifts, in 1958 O'Shaughnessy was granted the Knight Commander Order of St. Gregory by Pope Pius XII; in 1967 he was made a papal count.

When O'Shaughnssy died in 1973 his oldest son, John O'Shaughnessy, became president of the foundation.

ARD SCHULZE

EPRENEUR

Schulze takes out a
d mortgage on his
and starts an
nics business.

NDING BANKRUPTCY

) Dangerously close to
uptcy, Schulze borrows
y from his family,
ses his product line,
ceives a $100,000
credit — using his
ers' inventory as
eral.

WARS

) Schulze adds floor
and puts the sales
on salary in an effort to
ad-to-head with
nd Super Stores. His
etitor finally goes out
iness.

FFS

) Schulze gives the ax
ny senior employees in
ort to cut costs. Best
urpasses Circuit City to
ne the nation's largest
nics retailer.

Richard Schulze

RICHARD SCHULZE FOUNDED the Best Buy Corporation.

The St. Paul Central High School graduate learned about electronics in the Minnesota Air National Guard. After his discharge from the guard he became an independent manufacturer's representative and sold consumer electronics throughout a four-state area. After six years, he took out a second mortgage on his house and started his own electronics business.

In 1966 Schulze opened Sound of Music stores in nine locations. Sound of Music almost went bankrupt in 1980, but Schulze talked his creditors into extending further credit. Having weathered that storm, Schulze moved forward by opening Best Buy Super Stores in Burnsville and in six other Upper Midwest locations. But Highland Super Stores and other retail chain stores began to cut into Best Buy's market share, and Schulze saw his company's earnings drop 64 percent.

In response to the crisis Shulze added more floor space, kept the floor fully stocked, and put the sales people on salary instead of commission. This created a more shopper-friendly environment, and Best Buy started to recoup earnings; Highland Super Stores went out of business.

Circuit City still owned a majority of the marketplace, however. To combat this giant, Schulze opened larger stores with more products and interactive technology. The plan boosted market share, and Best Buy pulled closer to its rival. Meanwhile, earnings dropped, and Schulze suffered a tremendous personal loss when his parents died eight months apart in 1997.

The stress took its toll and Schulze finally took a two-week vacation. He returned with a new plan. Customer service would be improved and the shareholders would see the results. He brought in a consulting company that found Best Buy had expanded beyond its capacity. The consultants found that many senior executives, although they had been valuable for decades, were no longer needed. Schulze made the necessary changes. Before long, Best Buy had surpassed Circuit City to became the nation's largest retailer of consumer electronics.

Schulze resigned as chief executive officer in 2002. He is still the chairman of the board of Best Buy.

James Ford Bell

BORN IN PHILADELPHIA, Pennsylvania, James Ford Bell moved with his family to Minnesota when he was a boy. His father took a job with the Washburn Milling Company and in 1888 assumed leadership of the company. The elder Bell worked tirelessly to expand his control of the flour market, and the company grew rapidly.

James attended the University of Minnesota, graduating in 1901 with a bachelor's degree in chemistry. He followed in his father's footsteps and went to work at the Washburn Crosby Milling Company. He eventually became president of that company and was instrumental in completing mergers with other Mid-western mills to create General Mills. Soon General Mills was the largest flour miller in the world, controlling twenty-seven companies in sixteen states. Under Bell's leadership, General Mills continued to expand throughout the Depression and war years, making use of innovative marketing strategies and developing new products to satisfy a growing demand for easy-to-use cereals and mixes.

Bell also took an avid interest in ex-ploring the history of the industry in which he had become a world leader. In the course of these inquiries he amassed a considerable collection of books dating from the earliest years of European contact with other peoples around the world. In 1953 Bell donated 600 carefully chosen books to the University of Minnesota, which became the core of the James Ford Bell Library, a collection that today in-cludes more than 20,000 items.

Under Bell's leadership, General Mills continued to expand throughout the Depression and war years, making use of innovative marketing strategies and developing new products to satisfy a growing demand for easy-to-use cereals and mixes.

JAMES FORD BELL

MOVE TO MINNESOTA

(1887) Bell moves to Minnesota from Philadelphia, Pennsylvania, at the age of nine. His father becomes manager of the Washburn Crosby Milling Company.

UNIVERSITY OF MINNESOTA

(1901) Bell receives his bachelor's degree in chemistry from the University of Minnesota and goes to work for his father at the milling company.

GENERAL MILLS

(1928) As the founder of General Mills, Bell consolidates several midwest milling operations.

AMERICAN WILDLIFE FOUNDATION

(1931–1938) A man of many interests, Bell researches the delta wetlands in Manitoba, Canada, and establishes the American Foundation. It has been renamed the Delta Waterfowl Foundation.

MINNEAPOLIS INSTITUTE OF ARTS

(1960s and 1970s) His collection of early American silver is donated to the Institute of Arts. The Charleston Rooms are donated to the museum in memory of his parents.

Carl Pohlad

THE SON OF A RAILWAY brakeman, Pohlad grew up in Junction Valley, Iowa. As a youth he washed clothes and cleaned homes with other members of his family to scrape by financially. After his high school graduation he moved to the West Coast, where he attended Gonzaga University on a football scholarship and became a starting end on the football team. Pohlad quit school after his last football season, however, to sell used cars. He was drafted into the army and served courageously during World War II. When he returned from the war Pohlad went back to Iowa to pursue a career in business.

In 1949 Pohlad went to work with his brother-in-law at Marquette National Bank in Minneapolis. He was named president and chief executive officer in 1955. He went on to develop a soft-drink bottling empire and also invested heavily in airlines and real estate.

Business success aside, over the years Pohlad has been deeply involved in the community. In 1960 he cofounded the Minneapolis Boys Club, and he was finance director for Hubert Humphrey's 1970 senatorial campaign. He had long expressed an interest in owning a pro sports team, but attempts to purchase the San Francisco Giants and later the Philadelphia Eagles fell through. When it seemed that the Minnesota Twins were going to be moved after the 1984 season Pohlad purchased the local team from longtime owner Calvin Griffith. The two men met at home plate on June 22 before the start of a game and transferred ownership of the team. The Twins would go on to win World Series Championships in 1987 and 1991.

The Twins struggled during the late 1990s, however, and Pohlad lost friends when he seemed unduly eager to see the team disappear. The issue was contested in court and a Hennepin County judge issued an injunction forcing the Twins to fulfill their Metrodome lease. Major League Baseball eventually decided against contraction, and Pohlad remains not only the majority owner of the Twins, but also one of the team's biggest fans.

In recognition of his contributions to the local business community, Pohlad was inducted into the Minnesota Business Hall of Fame in 1983. A few years later he was given the Distinguished Service Award by the city of Minneapolis, and the next year he was elected to the Minnesota Executive Hall of Fame. Pohlad is on the Forbes 400 list of wealthiest Americans.

CARL POHLAD

WORLD WAR II

(1941–1945) As an infantryman in the U.S. Army Pohlad earns several decorations.

BANK SHARES INC.

(1955) Pohlad is named president of the Minneapolis financial company that also owns a holding company, Marquette National Bank.

BOYS CLUB

(1960) He is a cofounder of the Minneapolis Boys Club.

MINNESOTA TWINS

(1984) With lifelong baseball man Calvin Griffin ready to move the team, Pohlad makes an offer to purchase the Twins.

HONORED CITIZEN

(1983-87) Pohlad is inducted into the Minnesota Business Hall of Fame in 1983. A few years later he is given the Distinguished Service Award by the city of Minneapolis, and the next year he is elected to the Minnesota Executive Hall of Fame.

THE MUSICIANS

Bob Dylan

BOBBY ZIMMERMAN WAS BORN in Duluth, Minnesota, in 1941. The family later moved to Hibbing, where Bob, in his early teens, started playing the piano in his parents' living room to the sound of rock and roll. He later performed with several local bands, although his most notable performance might well have been at the Hibbing High School talent show, where his gyrations at the piano drove the audience hysterical with laughter.

Dylan moved to Minneapolis in the fall of 1959 and enrolled at the University of Minnesota, though he spent most of his time studying the works of Hank Williams, Woody Guthrie, and Robert Johnson, and performed their tunes (and sometimes his own) at the Ten O'clock Scholar and the Purple Onion.

Dylan went to Greenwich Village in 1960 to be closer to the folk scene, and on April 14, 1961, he performed his first paid New York show, sharing the bill with John Lee Hooker. Legendary producer John Hammond Jr. heard one of his shows, and before long Hammond had produced Dylan's first recording, *Bob Dylan*, which was released on the Columbia Records label in the spring of 1962.

But Dylan's second album, *The Free Wheelin' Bob Dylan*, was a true revelation. It contained "Blowin' in the Wind," "A Hard Rain's Gonna Fall," "Don't Think Twice, It's Alright," and nine other originals, and established Dylan as the greatest poet-songwriter of his generation. Some Dylan songs, among them "Blowin' in the Wind" and "Mr. Tambourine Man," became hits for Joan Baez; The Byrds; Peter, Paul, and Mary; and other recording artists. In fact, Dylan's genius

and popularity at the time was so great that when the Beatle's landed in New York, they requested that he pay a visit to their hotel.

In 1965, with *Bringin' It All Back Home*, Dylan shocked his folk-rock fans by recording with an electric band. Yet the album was very strong and contained masterpieces—"Mr. Tambourine Man," and "Subterranean Homesick Blues," among others. *Highway 61 Revisited* and *Blonde on Blonde*, released in the following months, were equally distinguished.

In light of the supernova that was his early career, it was perhaps inevitable that Dylan seemed to lose his way, if not his unconventionality, in the following years. After a motorcycle accident in 1966, he removed himself from the public eye for five years, and in the next decade developed a reputation for confused and erratic performances and recordings. On the other hand, the 1974 *Planet Waves* became his first number-one album, and *Blood on the Tracks*, released the same year, is considered one of his best.

In the course of time, Dylan recorded with Mark Knopfler, The Band, and the Travelling Wilburys, an ensemble that also included George Harrison, Roy Orbison, and Tom Petty. And at an age when many of his contemporaries had long since thrown in the towel, Dylan began to hit the road for months at a time, touring all but indefatigably, year in and year out.

In 1997 Dylan won three Grammys for his album *Time Out of Mind*, including Album of the Year, and an Oscar for Best Song with "Things Have Changed" from the soundtrack of the movie *Wonder Boys*.

The Andrews Sisters

SISTERS MAXINE, PATTY, AND LAVERNE Andrews were born in Mound, Minnesota, in the second decade of the twentieth century. The girls enjoyed singing together from an early age and worked out their own arrangements of popular songs. As their repertoire developed, they began to perform at fairs, in vaudeville shows, and at night clubs, sometimes touring in their father's Buick for months at a time.

The singing sisters found steady work in 1936 when they were asked to perform with Leon Belasco's orchestra in New York. When Decca A&R vice president Dave Kapp heard them perform on the radio, he was so impressed that he invited the Andrews Sisters to his office, later signing them to a recording contract. Their big break finally came in 1937 with the hit tune "Bei Mir Bist Du Shön," which sold 350,00 copies and held the number-one slot for five weeks on the Billboard charts.

Other hits soon followed, including "Ferryboat Serenade." The sisters were in such demand that Hollywood beckoned, and in 1940 they appeared in *Argentine Nights*, the first of sixteen movie appearances. During World War II, they became even more successful with such hits as "Boogie Woogie Bugle Boy," "Shoo-Shoo Baby," "Pistol Packin' Mama," "Hot Time in the Town of Berlin," and "Don't Fence Me In." Their performances for U.S. servicemen were much anticipated.

In 1949, Patty's solo "I Can Dream Can't I?" became a number-one hit, and a year later "I Want to be Loved" once again topped the charts. Patty left the group in 1954 to perform solo, but she returned to the fold two years later. By that time, however, a new generation of performers was spreading the new music gospel of rock and roll, and the Andrews Sisters never again returned to their former glory.

Yet the Andrews Sisters sold 90 million records during their career, and their return to Broadway in 1974 in the World War II musical *Over There*, directly on the heals of Bette Midler's wonderful remake of "Boogie Woogie Bugle Boy," introduced a new generation of listeners to their inimitable blending of luscious voices.

Maxine (l), Patty and LaVerne Andrews

PRINCE

DIRTY MIND

(1980) This raw piece of original work by Prince was recorded in his home studio. His father was a jazz pianist and played at Minneapolis striptease clubs.

1999

(1983) The hit singles from this double album are "Little Red Corvette," "Delirious," and "1999." They provide the real groove that makes this a rock-and-roll timepiece.

PURPLE RAIN

(1984) A soundtrack for the movie, *Purple Rain* reached number one on the Billboard charts. The movie, starring Prince, Morris Day, and Apollonia Kotero, was number-one at the box office as well.

SIGN OF THE TIMES

(1987) Prince comes of age with this rock classic. Perhaps his best album, *Sign of the Times* features Sheila E. on percussion, Eric Leeds on sax, and, of course, Prince on guitar.

VH1 POLL

(1998) In a poll of 600 of his peers, Prince is voted the seventeenth most influential artist in the history of rock and roll.

NEW GROOVE

(2004–2005) After several years of distribution and studio problems, Prince finally cuts a deal with Columbia/Sony Records. His next release, *Musicology*, wins two Grammy Awards.

Prince

PRINCE ROGER NELSON was born June 7, 1958, in Minneapolis. He was raised in Minneapolis, where his father was a jazz musician. His parents divorced when he was seven, and Prince began hammering out tunes on the piano his father left behind. That was the beginning of a lifelong exploration of musical expression that would eventually bring Prince to the very top of the heap among rock and pop musicians.

During his high school years Prince played in several bands, including Champagne with bassist Andre Cymone. Eventually he recorded a demo tape and Warner Brothers liked what they heard. At the age of nineteen he signed with Warner to both produce and record three albums.

These early albums were moderately successful, but it was only in 1982, with the album called *1999*, that Prince reached superstar status. *1999* was a smashing success on the Billboard charts, and MTV played the songs "1999" and "Little Red Corvette" almost every hour. Two years later Prince released the popular film *Purple Rain*, and the following spring he had the unprecedented

distinction of holding title to the top single, the top album, and the top film in the same week. Prince's next two albums, *Around the World in a Day* (1985) and *Parade* (1986), hit number one as well. *Sign of the Times* was released in 1987 and although not as pop-oriented as his previous two albums, many consider this album to be his very best.

Prince also wrote material for other artists: The Bangles had a hit with "Manic Monday," Sheena Easton with "Sugar Walls," and Sheila E. with "Erotic City."

In 1992 Prince signed a six-album deal with Warner, but relations between the artist and studio were strained, and throughout the 1990s Prince's career took the same shape as his new name—a strange and indecipherable glyph.

In recent times Prince has once again been recording with success, and his introduction to the Rock and Roll Hall of Fame in March 2004, in his first year of eligibility, found the rocker in the midst of a new era of creativity.

While still in high school, Prince recorded a demo tape and Warner Brothers liked what they heard.

At the age of nineteen he signed with Warner to both produce and record three albums.

Lester Young

LESTER YOUNG WAS BORN in Mississippi in 1909, but by 1920 his family had moved to Minneapolis. His father, a musician, taught all of his children instruments and then formed a family band that toured throughout the Midwest. Young tried several instruments before settling on the alto saxophone. Following a family dispute, Young left the family band to tour with Art Bronson's Bostonians, Walter Page's Blue Devils, and other units, but he eventually re-settled in Minneapolis, where he played at the Nest Club, which was then famous for its swinging atmosphere.

In later years, Young made Kansas City his base but returned to Minnesota regularly to perform. It was during these years that he began an association with the Count Basie Band that would eventually lead to national recognition.

Young's style was smoother and airier than the one made popular by Coleman Hawkins, however, and brilliant though he was, many fans preferred the squeaking, shouting riffs of older reedmen. But younger musicians appreciated his innovative approach, and in 1944, following a reunion with the Basie Band, Young won the award for Best Tenor Saxophone from *Down Beat Magazine*. By this time he had also developed an unusually deep rapport with Billy Holiday, the finest female vocalist of the era, and things were going well for him, but in the fall of 1944 Young was drafted into the U.S. Army. His experiences in the military were dreadful. He was court-martialed for drug abuse and spent time in detention before being released the following year.

Young continued to perform brilliantly, if erratically, during the postwar years, and he inspired a new generation of tenor players, including Stan Getz, Sonny Rollins, and John Coltrane, but lapses in energy and innovation became more frequent with the passage of time, while his bouts with alcohol became more debilitating.

Young died in New York in 1959.

Dominick Argento

ONE OF AMERICA'S FOREMOST composers of classical music, Dominick Argento has lived in Minnesota since 1958, when he joined the music faculty at the University of Minnesota. He taught composition at the university for thirty-nine years, all the while adding to his composition list and his reputation.

Locally in Minnesota, his commissions include pieces for the Saint Paul Chamber Orchestra, the Dale Warland Singers, the Civic Orchestra of Minneapolis, the Schubert Club, and the Minnesota Orchestra. In the 1960s, he worked closely with Sir Tyrone Guthrie, composing incidental music for several Guthrie theatrical productions. He was a cofounder of Minneapolis's Center Opera and wrote several operas for that company, which later evolved into the Minnesota Opera. In 1997, he was given a lifetime appointment as Composer Laureate to the Minnesota Orchestra.

He is best known for his vocal works. His song cycles have received worldwide attention, and his operas have been performed by the Chicago Lyric Opera, the New York City Opera, and the Stockholm Royal Opera, as well as broadcast on PBS *Great Performances*. Argento received the Pulitzer Prize in 1975 for a song cycle commissioned by the Schubert Club, *From the Diary of Virginia Woolf*. He received the 2004 Grammy for Best Classical Contemporary Composition for Frederica von Stade's recording of his *Casa Guidi* song cycle.

LESTER YOUNG

STYLE DEVELOPS

(1926–1935) During his years in Minneapolis, Lester begins playing the tenor sax; he is deeply influenced by Louis Armstrong and also by the white, C-melody saxophonist Frankie Trumbauer. He plays regularly at the Kit Kat, the Nest, the Cotton, and other North Side Minneapolis clubs.

THE PRES' AND LADY DAY

(1937-1938) Lester records the first of many timeless classics with Billy Holiday, and they also confer enduring "titles" on one another.

THE COUNT

(1943) Lester returns to the Basie Band, finally receiving the widespread exposure that will catapult him to the top of the tenor heap.

DOMINICK ARGENTO

OPERA

(1950s) Argento serves as musical director of Baltimore's Hilltop Opera.

UNIVERSITY OF MINNESOTA

(1958) The esteemed Argento is hired at the University of Minnesota to teach music theory and composition.

GLOBAL SUCCESS

(1963–1967) Argento's *Christopher Sly* (1963), *The Masque of Angels* (1964), and *The Shoemaker's Holiday* (1967) are performed in New York. Meanwhile, several of his operas reach the stage in Sweden and Germany.

PULITZER

(1975) Argento receives the Pulitzer Prize for music for his composition *From the Diary of Virginia Woolf*.

HONOR

(1997) Argento is chosen as the Composer Laureate of the Minnesota Orchestra.

Jimmy "Jam" Harris III & Terry Lewis

THIS PROLIFIC SONGWRITING and producing team has been nominated for seven Grammy Awards. Jimmy Jam Harris attended Minneapolis Central High School. Lewis went to Minneapolis North. Together with other musicians, the two formed the band FlyteTime, with Harris playing keyboards and Lewis on bass. The band later changed its name to The Time and toured as backup band with Prince in the early 1980s.

Prince produced two albums for The Time, but before long Harris and Lewis had become eminent producers in their own right, recording smash hits with Gladys Knight, Patti Austin, Thelma Houston and Klymaxx. With the Janet Jackson album *Control* (1986), they hit Platinum-plus. The album contained four number-one hits and made Jackson a superstar. It also earned Harris and Lewis a Grammy for Producers of the Year. Since that time, the duo has produced several more best-selling albums with Jackson, and also worked studio magic with Boyz II Men, Luther Vandross, Mary J. Blige, Shaggy, Patti LaBelle, Maria Carey, and

Vanessa Williams, among many others. All in all, they have produced over 100 albums and singles that have achieved Gold or Platinum sales.

In 1997 the duo formed FlyteTime records and got off to a very good start with the soundtrack to *How Stella Got Her Groove Back*. They also signed a deal to produce records for Arista on a contract basis. Often one step ahead of the curve in a fickle industry, Harris and Lewis have continued to reinvent themselves successfully, and are the only contemporary producers to have put out consistent number-one hit records in three successive decades.

In the summer of 2004, Lewis and Harris moved Flyte Time studios to Los Angeles. They have recently been honored with a star on the Hollywood Walk of Fame.

Harris and Lewis recorded smash hits with Gladys Knight, Patti Austin, Thelma Houston, and Klymaxx. With the Janet Jackson album *Control* (1986), they hit Platinum-plus.

Jimmy "Jam" Harris (l) and Terry Lewis

YANNI WAS BORN and raised in Kalamata, Greece, a region hitherto mostly famous for its olives. He moved with his family to Minnesota and graduated from the University of Minnesota in 1976 with a degree in psychology. As a student he lived in a dorm on campus and played the piano in the first floor lounge late at night.

After playing with several local bands, Yanni began devising keyboard solo shows, some of which were accompanied by lasers. He performed shows in Florida, Chicago, and at First Avenue in Minneapolis, but the reaction was mixed, and Yanni joined the band Chameleon, which played to large crowds at ballrooms during the early 1980s.

When Chameleon disbanded, Yanni took on jobs writing and recording music for advertising companies in Minneapolis. He dropped the lucrative career to write and record his own music while living in his sister's basement. He produced and recorded several albums.

In 1985 a radio in New Jersey began to give airtime to Yanni's 1980 album *Optimystique*, and before long Yanni had signed a recording deal with Private Music. He recorded *Keys to Imagination* (1986) for the label at his home studio in Brooklyn Park, and the album won the Best New Age Album award that year.

Yanni's first Grammy-nominated album *Dare to Dream* (1992), contained the track "Aria," which British Airways used as a theme song. *In My Time*, a collection of mellow piano pieces, was also nominated for a Grammy Award and went Platinum. But the highlight of Yanni's career took place in 1993, when he returned to Greece to performed three resplendent shows at the Acropolis. The album *Yanni: Live At The Acropolis*, was a spectacular success. The CD has remained on the charts almost continuously since its release, and the music video is a perennial best seller.

Yanni has performed recently to broadcast audiences around the world at the Taj Majal and China's Forbidden City. He also continues to record regularly. His recent album *Ethnicity* explores a wide spectrum of musical idioms from around the world.

The Replacements

ALTHOUGH THEIR ALBUM *Let It Be* (1984) was included in *The Rolling Stone 200: the definitive library of the best albums ever made*, the Replacements have the dubious distinction of being perhaps the most highly esteemed band of the 1980s never to have reached the mainstream.

Formed by brothers Tommy and Bob Stinson, Chris Mars, and Paul Westerberg in 1979, they were influenced, like most punk rockers, by the Ramones and the Sex Pistols. Westerberg was a Bob Dylan fan, and the band drew upon the music of John Lennon.

The band began their career in Minneapolis as The Impediments. Having been banned from a venue for performing drunk, they returned a few weeks later under a new name—The Replacements. In the early years they were often compared to the famous Minneapolis group Hüsker Dü, and when that band folded they took over the local spotlight. Their 1983 album *Hootenanny* was given airtime on many college radio stations, and the band began to develop a national audience. On the strength of the follow-up release, *Let It Be* (1984), which was filled with cutting-edge alternative rock, the Replacements received several offers from major labels.

They signed a contract with Sire, and released another album, *Tim*, in 1985. It was produced by ex-Ramones drummer Tommy Erdelyi, and is considered by many to be their best.

Mainstream success appeared to be right around the corner, but the band's unruly behavior made them a continuing embarrassment to their label and their fans, and their heavy touring schedule was also taking its toll. Bob Stinson, the band's lead guitarist and most extreme reveler, was fired. (He died of a drug overdose in 1995.) The trio of Westerberg, Mars, and Tommy Stinson went on to record another gem, *Please to Meet Me* (1987) in Memphis. Bob "Slim" Dunlap later joined the band on tour to provide them with a dependable lead guitar player.

The Replacements' next offering, *Don't Tell a Soul* (1989), contained the band's only semi-hit, "I'll Be You," which reached number 51 on the Billboard charts. *All Shook Down* (1990) was recorded largely by Westerberg using studio musicians. Clearly the band was on its last legs. Chris Mars left the group in 1991, and the Replacements broke up less than a year later.

Paul Westerberg (l), Tommy Stinson and Chris Mars

THE EXPLORERS

Charles Lindbergh

CHARLES LINDBERGH WAS THE first person to fly an airplane across the Atlantic Ocean.

Born on February 4, 1902, in Detroit, Michigan, Lindbergh grew up on a farm in Little Falls, Minnesota, where his father, a Swedish immigrant, had become a U.S. congressman. He enrolled at the University of Wisconsin to study engineering, but caught the aviation bug and dropped out after two years to pursue a career as a pilot.

In 1922 Lindbergh began taking classes at Ray Page's Flying School in Lincoln, Nebraska. By July the show-boating Lindbergh was barnstorming throughout the Midwest, as a pilot, parachute jumper and wing walker.

Lindbergh received his formal training in San Antonio, Texas, with the Air Service of the U.S. Army. He was commissioned a second lieutenant in the reserves, and went to work for Robertson Aircraft flying mail from St. Louis to Chicago.

A few years earlier a New York City hotel owner had offered a $25,000 prize to the first pilot to fly solo across the Atlantic from New York to Paris. Several pilots had already died in efforts to complete the long flight, but Lindbergh felt he could meet the challenge. He and his plane, the *Spirit of St. Louis*, rolled down Roosevelt Field in New York on May 20, 1927. More than half the gross weight of the plane was gasoline.

On the morning following Lindbergh's departure his plane was sighted off the coast of Ireland. News traveled fast, and when he landed at Le Bourget Field near Paris, France, Lindbergh became an instant hero. The trip had taken thirty-three hours and thirty minutes. Lindbergh received parades in New York and Little Falls and was awarded the Medal of Honor.

In 1929 Lindbergh married Anne Morrow, the daughter of an eminent ambassador, and he taught her how to fly. They set the transcontinental speed record together, wrote books about their travels, and became a national treasure as a couple. Their star was dimmed by the tragic kidnapping of their first son in 1932, however, and it was seriously tarnished when Lindbergh accepted the German Medal of Honor from Hermann Göring in 1938. He was accused of being a Nazi sympathizer and was forbidden to fly in Europe.

Lindbergh opposed America's entry into World War II, but later flew training missions as a civilian for the Allies in the Pacific theater. In 1954 he was named brigadier general of the U.S. Air Force.

Late in life Lindbergh was involved in the space program, and he was also an avid environmentalist. He moved to Hawaii, where he died in 1974.

WILL STEGER

Will Steger

WILL STEGER GREW UP on the outskirts of Minneapolis, yet he spent many a summer in the wilderness of Canada, specifically the Yukon region. These experiences sparked the desire to undertake extraordinary treks, and once he had finished his education, Steger lost little time in doing so.

His first and most spectacular arctic effort came in 1986, when Steger led an expedition by dogsled to the North Pole. His team became only the second group in history to do this successfully. (Admiral Robert E. Perry and his men had been to the North Pole in 1909.) Two years later he accomplished the longest unsupported dogsled trip in history, a 1,600-mile south-north traverse of Greenland.

Steger later set his sights on the Antarctic and the South Pole. In 1990 he and his six-person expedition trekked across the 4,000-mile continent in 220 days. A Soviet welcoming committee greeted Steger and his international team of explorers at the end of the trip. A few years later he completed a dogsled traverse of the Arctic Ocean from Siberia to Ellesmere Island. For these and other accomplishments Steger was named National Geographic's first explorer-in-residence in 1996.

Steger is the author of four books: *Over the Top of the World, Crossing Antarctica, North to the Pole,* and *Saving the Earth.* He lives in Ely, Minnesota.

Ann Bancroft

AS AN ELEMENTARY SCHOOLTEACHER, Ann Bancroft encouraged her students to be adventurous. It must have come as no great surprise to them when she joined Will Steger on his North Pole expedition in 1986.

The Arctic explorer grew up in Mendota Heights, and developed a taste for the outdoors while accompanying her parents on their frequent trips to the Boundary Waters Canoe Area Wilderness. She attended St. Paul Academy and Henry Sibley High School, and received a degree in physical education from the University of Oregon.

When Will Steger set off for the North Pole on March 6, 1986, Bancroft was with him. With the dogs from Ely, Minnesota, leading the way, they started out across the Northwest Territories. Bancroft's responsibilities during the journey included overseeing medical supplies and taking photographs for *National Geographic*. When the party reached their goal some eight weeks later, Bancroft became the first known woman in history to cross the ice at the North Pole.

Soon Bancroft was planning expeditions of her own. In 1993 she led a group of four women on a 660 mile trek to the

South Pole, becoming the first all-women expedition to do so, while Bancroft herself became the first woman to have reached both of the poles. Seven years later, she and Norwegian Liv Arnesen set out to become the first women to ski across the entire Antarctic landmass from coast to coast.

They began the adventure on November 13, 2000, with schoolchildren worldwide tracking the 1,700-mile journey on the Internet. On February 11, 2001, they reached the edge of the Ross Ice Shelf, becoming the first women in history to ski across the continent. Although they had hoped to ski and sail the remaining 460 miles across the ice to a ship waiting at McMurdo Station on Cape Evans, the winds didn't cooperate, and they were forced to call in a ski plane to pick them up.

Bancroft now lives in Scandia, Minnesota, while traveling widely to promote educational activities that inspire young women to succeed at what they set out to do. She has been the recipient of numerous awards, including *Ms. Magazine's* Woman of the Year for 1987. She was inducted into the National Women's Hall of Fame in 1995.

THE ARTISTS
Charles Schulz

CHARLES SCHULZ IS A HOUSEHOLD name throughout the world thanks to his well-loved comic strip, *Peanuts*.

Born in Minneapolis in 1922, Schulz grew up in St. Paul and attended St. Paul Central High School, where he earned the nickname "Sparky" after the horse in *Barney Google*. Neither of his parents had received schooling beyond the third grade, and in later life Charles looked back fondly to the simplicity and affection that characterized his childhood years. An unusually bright child, Charles skipped a grade in elementary school, and spent his high school years as an unpopular and inconspicuous student. To the end of his life he felt the sting occasioned when the editor of the Central High yearbook rejected a batch of his drawings.

When his mother died at the age of forty-eight, a few days before he was shipped off to World War II in Europe, Schulz's world was irrevocably shattered. The feelings of worthlessness, loss, anxiety, and frustration he felt at the time would later reappear in lighter forms to animate his famous comic strip.

After serving in the army during World War II, Schulz created a comic strip called *Lil' Folks*, focusing on the foibles and common concerns of children. The main characters were Charlie Brown, Lucy, Linus, and Snoopy. It was featured in the *St. Paul Pioneer Press* and later the *Saturday Evening Post*. Schulz eventually took his comic to New York City and presented it to United Features. A deal was reached, and the name of the strip was changed to *Peanuts*.

Peanuts became a huge success, appearing in more than 2,000 newspapers worldwide. As the 1960s wore on, and the nation sank ever more deeply into problems both overseas and at home, the childlike but strangely "adult" world Schultz created took on added luster. Paperback reprints of the cartoon strip became wildly popular, eventually selling more than 300 million copies, and there were Broadway shows, feature films, and more than thirty television specials based on the comic strip. Snoopy toys, Charlie Brown sweatshirts, and other product tie-ins brought United Artists over a billion dollars a year in revenue and made Charles Schulz the richest popular artist of his time. He appeared regularly on *Forbes'* yearly list of the ten highest-paid entertainers in the industry, while theologians and semiologists wrote scholarly tomes dissecting the deep moral significance of his creations. All the while Schulz continued to draw his strip by hand, day after day, with a quill-tipped pen, and without a team of assistants.

Schulz became ill in 1998 with colon cancer, and announced his retirement. His last *Peanuts* comic strip appeared in papers on February 12, 2000. He died in his sleep that very night.

"I don't know the meaning of life," Schulz once said. "I don't know why we are here. I think life is full of anxieties and fears and tears. It has a lot of grief in it, and it can be very grim. And I do not want to be the one who tries to tell somebody else what life is all about. To me it's a complete mystery."

WARREN MACKENZIE WAS BORN in Kansas City, Missouri, on February 16, 1924. He studied painting at the Art Institute of Chicago before joining the army during World War II. He returned to Chicago after the war, and, finding the painting classes full, he began to study ceramics. It would become his life's work.

In 1948 MacKenzie moved to St. Paul, Minnesota, to teach. His potting reached a new level during a two-year apprenticeship in St. Ives, England, with Bernard Leach, the man largely responsible for bringing the Japanese tradition in potting to the West. MacKenzie returned from England in 1953 to set up his own studio on a farm outside Stillwater, and to begin teaching ceramics at the University of Minnesota. He had his first exhibition at the Walker Art Center a year later.

Following in the footsteps of Leach and Japanese master Shoji Hamada, MacKenzie's approach to ceramics has remained utilitarian throughout his career. He intends that his creations be used, not merely admired. To this end he produces large quantities of bowls, mugs, plates, casseroles, platters and vases, which he offers for sale at reasonable prices in the showroom of his rural studio. Yet the unusual subtlety and beauty of his wheel-thrown creations has made them widely sought-after by collectors, and his works have frequently been selected for touring shows. They can also be seen in the permanent collections of galleries and museums from Tokyo to Finland. In fact, in a survey conducted by *Ceramics Monthly* in 1981, Mackenzie was chosen as one of the twelve best potters in the world.

The prestigious Kodansha Publishing of Tokyo put out *Warren MacKenzie: American Potter*, in 1981.

Warren Mackenzie

Joe (l), Robert and Jim Hautman

The Hautman Brothers

WILDLIFE ARTISTS JOE, BOB, AND TIM Hautman have won more than forty state and federal duck stamp awards, and between them the trio has won seven of the last thirteen Federal Duck Stamp competitions.

The Hautmans' story has been featured in leading publications, including *Time*, *USA Today*, and *Sports Illustrated*. The brothers' art has been displayed in the White House. They were chosen to create three wildlife paintings in a new Landmark print series. Joe's painting of canvasbacks flying past the Statue of Liberty was the first of the Habitat 2000 Landmark Series. The following year Bob's painting of tundra swans on Sedge Island on Barnegat Bay was released. And in 2002, a painting featuring an autumn scene

of wood ducks at the Delaware Water Gap completed the wildlife series of collectable state duck stamp prints.

In 2003 the Hautmans were asked to create a print for the one-hundredth birthday of the National Wildlife Refuge System. The Hautmans' print "A Century of Conservation" features wildlife scenes from three different eras in the history of the refuge system. It was the first time the brothers had collaborated on a piece of art.

The brothers continue to make Minnesota their home. Joe, who worked for many years as a physicist before turning to art full-time, lives in Plymouth; Jim lives in Chaska, and Robert in Delano.

WANDA GAG

BIRTHPLACE

(1893) Wanda Gag is born on March 11 in New Ulm, Minnesota.

ART SCHOOLING

(1913–1917) Gag takes art classes at the St. Paul School of Art and the Minneapolis School of Art.

MILLIONS OF CATS

(1928) Gag is perhaps best remembered for writing and illustrating the popular children's book *Millions of Cats.*

FAIRY TALES

(1936) She translates and illustrates *Tales from Grimm.*

WONDERFUL ARTISTRY

(1938) Her illustrations appear in the book *Snow White and the Seven Dwarfs.*

A LOOK BACK

(1940) Gag wrote an autobiography, *Growing Pains,* in which she recounts her childhood in New Ulm.

Wanda Gag

THE ELDEST OF SEVEN children, Wanda Gag was born on March 11, 1893, and raised in New Ulm, Minnesota. Her parents were of Bohemian extraction, and her father painted murals on churches and public buildings in their hometown. Though Gag exhibited a talent for art as a child, her father died when she was only fifteen, and the family was soon almost destitute. Upon graduating from high school in 1914, Gag worked as a teacher in a country school. Later, while attending the St. Paul School of Art (1913–1914), and the Minneapolis School of Art (1914–1917), she helped support her family by selling illustrations to *The Minneapolis Journal.*

In 1917 Gag received a scholarship from the Arts Students' League and moved to New York City, where she supported herself by painting lampshades and doing fashion designs. In 1923 she abandoned her career in commercial art, which she felt was stifling her creativity, and moved to the country, where she worked in relative isolation on her own projects. It was not an easy life at first, but in 1926 some of her art was exhibited at the Weyhe Gallery in New York City. Two years later she began writing and illustrating children's books, which introduced her to a far wider audience.

Millions of Cats is the most famous of Gag's ten books, although *ABC Bunny* is also an enduring classic. Gag also translated several selections of Grimm fairy tales into English, and supplied the accompanying illustrations. As her success grew, she bought a farm in New Jersey and invited two of her younger siblings to live with her. She continued to paint and draw, eventually showing her work in such notable places as the Metropolitan Museum of Art, the Library of Congress, the British Museum in London, the Bibliotheque Nationale in Paris, and the Pushkin Museum in Moscow.

The quality of Gag's children's books may be suggested by the fact that she was twice runner-up for the Newbury Award, given to the author of an outstanding text for a children's book, and twice runner-up for the Caldecott Award, given to the top illustrator. Gag also wrote an autobiography, *Growing Pains: Diaries and Drawings for the Years 1908–1917,* in which she recounts her early years of poverty in New Ulm.

Gag died from cancer at the age of fifty-three.

LEROY NEIMAN

YOUTH

(1930s) LeRoy Neiman earned money as a boy painting advertisements on the windows of grocery stores in St. Paul.

ST. PAUL

(1946) As a student at the St. Paul Gallery and School of Art, Neiman studies with Clement Haupers.

FATEFUL ENCOUNTER

(1954) Neiman and Hugh Hefner both worked in the same office at Carson Pirie Scott in Chicago. When Hefner started *Playboy*, Neiman became a top illustrator for the magazine.

MINNEAPOLIS INSTITUTE OF ART

(1953) Neiman's "Idle Boats" wins first prize in the Twin City Show at the Minneapolis Institute of Art.

REACHING OUT TO YOUTH

(1976) Neiman produces a series of low-cost prints for Burger King in conjunction with the 1976 Olympics. When he was accused of "selling out" he replied that he wanted art to be made available to kids as poor as he had been as a youth.

POPULAR DEMAND

(2005) Neiman produces about one thousand paintings and prints a year.

ARTIST LEROY NEIMAN developed a colorful technique for capturing the flash and drama of sporting events from the Olympics to the Kentucky Derby.

Neiman was born in 1927 in St. Paul, Minnesota. Abandoned by his father at an early age, he earned money for the family by doing caricatures and painting advertisements on grocery story windows. He attended Washington High School, and also took classes at the Minnesota Museum of Art and the St. Paul Gallery and School of Art. He served in Europe during World War II, and then moved to Chicago to study at the Art Institute.

Neiman taught at the Chicago Art Institute during the 1950s while working as a free-lance illustrator for Carson Pirie Scott, and it was here that he met a young and ambitious copy writer named Hugh Hefner. Before long Neiman's flamboyant renderings were appearing regularly in *Playboy Magazine*.

In 1958 Neiman was given a monthly column in *Playboy*, "Man at His Leisure," and was sent around the world to paint golf tournaments, yachting competitions, big game hunts, and other glamorous events. His work gained new levels of exposure when he was hired to create images for the Olympics—a role he continued to perform for the next twenty years—and his lightning-quick technique has also been on display in computer-generated form at Super Bowl telecasts.

Neiman himself, with broad handlebar mustache, white suit, and thick cigar, has cultivated an image of one who enjoys "the good life," and his lack of standing in the fine arts community has not prevented him from selling more than 150,000 paintings, etchings, and lithographs over the years to individuals of similar tastes. With aesthetic panache and journalistic accuracy, he has painted many of the heroes of our time, from Muhammad Ali to Michael Johnson, from Frank Sinatra to Princess Grace, from Wilt Chamberlain to Bobby Hull.

Neiman recently donated $6 million to fund the construction of a LeRoy Neiman Center for Print Studies at Columbia University's School of Art.

LeRoy Neiman

Cass Gilbert

DURING A LONG and productive career as an architect, Cass Gilbert put his stamp on a wide variety of buildings, including the Minnesota State Capital, the United States Supreme Court Building, and the Woolworth Building, which dramatically redefined the shape and height of the skyscraper.

Gilbert was born in Zanesville, Ohio, in 1859. The family moved to St. Paul, where Gilbert began his career as a draftsman and carpenter's helper. This field of work aroused his interest, and in 1878 he enrolled in an architecture program at Massachusetts Institute of Technology, the first of its kind in the United States. A year later he toured Europe, making elaborate watercolor sketches of buildings and architectural details. Following his return, Gilbert was hired as a draftsman for the rising firm of McKim, Mead & White in New York City, and in 1881 he was chosen to open and manage a new office for the firm in St. Paul. Anticipated contracts with the railroads were slow to materialize, however, and the office was closed a year later. Gilbert stayed on, and for the next ten years he designed a number of homes, churches, and warehouses in the Twin Cities area. Architects were still considered a luxury at the time, however, and Gilbert often supplemented his income by selling watercolors.

His big break came when he won the competition to design a new capital building for the state. The resultant work, though not terribly original, was both handsome and suitably imposing. Gilbert's insistence that the exterior be sheathed in Georgia marble rather than local stone did not win him many friends locally, however; but by this time he had opened an office in New York City, and it was not long before he had won the competition to design the new U.S. Customs House there. Other commissions for major buildings followed, not only in New York City, but also in St. Louis, Detroit, and Washington—a trajectory of success that peaked when, in 1911, Gilbert was chosen to design the Woolworth Building. Topping out at fifty-five stories, this building pushed steel-frame construction to the limit. The Woolworth Building was completed in 1913 and remained the tallest building in the world until 1930. Richly decorated with colored terracotta neo-Gothic ornaments, it stands today as a wistful reminder of the role once played in architecture by fancy and historical allusion.

Gilbert died in 1935, and his reputation plummeted almost immediately, as glass-and-steel Bauhaus design came into vogue. Yet many of his buildings are still standing, and as new generations of architects re-evaluate the role of history and whimsy in urban design, Gilbert's work has once again become a subject for both study and admiration.

GORDON PARKS, AN AWARD WINNING photographer for *Life Magazine*, has written twelve books, directed several films, and composed musical scores.

Parks was born in Fort Scott, Kansas, in 1912. The youngest of 15 children, he had very loving parents who provided for their kids. When he was 15 his mother died, and he was sent to St. Paul to live with his sister and her husband. There was a disagreement between the two males and Parks ended up living on the street, riding trolley cars to stay warm during the cold winter nights.

Parks worked as a piano player in a brothel and as a busboy at the upscale Minnesota Club during these difficult years. He later took a job as a waiter on the Northern Pacific Railroad. It was while reading magazines left lying on the seats that Parks first took an interest in the art that would shape his life—photography.

Parks noticed that the great social photographers of the age—Ben Shahn, Dorothea Lange, Walker Evans and others—were exploring the world of poverty, a world he knew well. He purchased a camera and began taking pictures in the slums on the south side of Chicago. His first professional shoot, however, was for Frank Murphy's women's clothing store in St. Paul. This work led to other similar assignments in Chicago, and in 1942 Parks became the first photographer to receive a fellowship from the Julius Rosenwald Foundation.

Thus freed from the constraints of commercial work, Parks took up several short-lived documentary projects. By 1944 he had returned to fashion photography, moving to New York, where he was eventually hired by *Glamour* and *Vogue* to do freelance work. He also began photographing gangs in Harlem, and after showing the results to *Life Magazine*, he became the first black photographer on their staff. Parks became *Life's* foreign correspondent in 1949, and spent the next few years shooting in France, Italy, Portugal, and Spain.

He added another dimension to his creative life in 1963 with the publication of the novel *The Learning Tree*. Three years later Parks published his autobiography, *A Choice of Weapons*. He directed the film *Shaft* in 1971 and helped found *Essence* magazine in 1973.

Gordon
Parks

Mary Colter

MARY COLTER WAS BORN in Pittsburgh, Pennsylvania on April 4, 1869. The family settled in St. Paul, Minnesota, when Mary was eleven. Her interest in art developed while attending public schools in Saint Paul, from which she graduated at the age of fourteen. When her father died unexpectedly, Mary enrolled at the California School of Design in San Francisco, and at the same time apprenticed herself to a local architect. She returned to her family in St. Paul in 1892, at the age of twenty-three, to teach art at Mechanic Arts High School. A woman of wide-ranging intellect, Colter also gave lectures on world history at the University of Minnesota and studied archaeology in her spare time.

Colter's talents were eventually brought to the attention of the Fred Harvey Company, which operated hotels and concessions along the Santa Fe Railway. In 1902 they offered her a job as decorator of an Indian building that stood adjacent to a hotel they were building in Albuquerque. They were pleased with her work and three years later commissioned her to design an entire building to house Indian arts and crafts on the southern rim of the Grand Canyon.

In 1910 Colter was offered a permanent job as a designer, decorator, and architect for the Fred Harvey Company. For the next forty years, she worked on the design and interior decoration of many new buildings, bringing her sensitivity to Native American arts and her feel for natural materials and indigenous traditions to hotels, National Park buildings, and train stations throughout the American Southwest. La Fonda in Santa Fe; La Posada in Winslow, Arizona; the Watchtower at the Grand Canyon; and Los Angeles' Union Station are just a few of the buildings that still bear the stamp of her remarkable aesthetic gifts.

For forty years Colter worked on the design and interior decoration of many new buildings, bringing her sensitivity to Native American arts and her feel for natural materials and indigenous traditions to hotels, National Park buildings, and train stations throughout the American Southwest.

Epilogue

IT HAS BEEN A PLEASURE, BUT ALSO A CHALLENGE, to determine whom it would be most appropriate to include among those Minnesotans who have risen to national, if not world-wide fame. My decisions have been guided not only by intrinsic merit, but also by the desire to highlight individuals from a wide spectrum of pursuits, and from various eras of our state's history. Constraints of space have made it necessary to exclude individuals as noteworthy as Dr. Richard Varco, punk-rock tyros Hüsker Dü, and hockey legend John Mariucci, to mention only a few. My apologies go out to other deserving Minnesotans, past and present, who have not been included.

As I see it, part of the fun of a book like *Famous Minnesotans* lies in just this type of question, and debates will no doubt be heated with regard to the wisdom of some of my choices. A second volume of *Famous Minnesotans* is already in the works, however, and I would welcome suggestions from any quarter as to whom we might include. Send your recommendations to me at flynn442002@yahoo.com, and perhaps your favorite broadcaster, classical musician, politician, wrestler or business tycoon will be included in *Famous Minnesotans Volume II*.